God
I Am
So
Angry
With
You

Copyright © 2019 by Chepren Carter

All rights reserved. No part of this publication may be reproduced, distributed, or transmitted in any form or by any means, including photocopying, recording, or other electronic or mechanical methods, without the prior written permission of the publisher, Chepren Carter.

I have tried to recreate events locales and conversations from my memories of them. In order to maintain their anonymity in some instances I have changed the names of individuals and places. I may have changed some identifying characteristics and details such as physical properties, occupations, and places of residence.

ISBN-13: 978-1098902599

Table of Contents

Acknowledgements i
Foreword ii
My Lord, Why? 1
The Dream 22
Break it Down 43
Lord, Check Please 88
How Must I Cope 104
Lord Who Are You 122
God Where Are You 138
My Relationship With My Heavenly Father 150
Lord Help Me 179
Lord I Want Revenge 211
Lord I Know You Love Me 224
Revelations 246

Acknowledgements

It is because of you that I took another breath. It is because of you that I took another step. Without you, I know life would truly have no meaning. I love you my dear children Xavier, Joshua, Shelyce, Jalen, Justice, Trinity, Titus, and Christian.

Foreword

Why does God allow suffering? Why does He allow unbearable pain while at times silent to our cries? These are common questions for believers and non-believers alike, and few have been able to articulate the answer. God is all-knowing, all-present, and all-powerful, but somehow, people are still put through seasons of suffering, some so painful that ending it all doesn't seem so far-fetched and doesn't feel so wrong. Add to that the whispers from demons who cheer you on, nudging you effortlessly toward the edge of the cliff, and thoughts that have never before entered your mind are now countless. One can only answer these hard questions after walking through the suffering, crawling on the ground, and bearing oneself with utmost honesty and transparency at a holy place set aside only for the broken and the Creator. No one else is invited to such a gathering.

Author Chepren Carter has been in these dark places where light is snuffed out and breathing is impossible. She stood face to face in prayer with God, asking Him questions that were filled with hurt, shame, and anger. Why? Why me? However, she pressed through it all and rose victoriously, with the power that is contained in forgiveness and grace, in understanding who we are and who God is. In her brilliantly written novel *God I'm So Angry With You*, Chepren takes the reader's hand and gracefully walks them through each step of her season, promising never to let go, just as God never let go of her. We suffer for His glory so that we can help others who are still on their journey—lost, confused, and broken. Chepren gives hope through her words, encouragement through her voice, and wisdom that allows us a glimpse of the magnificence of who God truly is.

I can say without a doubt that *God I'm So Angry With You* is a must read for all audiences from all backgrounds. This masterfully written book is relatable in its honesty, graceful in its story, and exudes a pure love that points not to our circumstances, but rather to the One who loves us more than we'll ever know.

- Russ Womack, Author of *Orange*

Chapter 1

My Lord, Why?

"When life gives you lemons, you make lemonade". Shaking my head, I wonder if all hell has broken loose in "Life's" life. A vapid expression to encourage, to ignite and possibly motivate to help you pick yourself up and move forward when every part of your world is coming down around you. A cliché I've heard used in stimulating a piece of the mind to try and take just one more step can't even make me look in any direction. I'm left wondering how to fix this mess that I'm in. This hurt that's now trapped in my heart. This ache shut up in my bones. I know that something is wrong, but I'm not sure exactly what it is.

There isn't one clear thought. My head is spinning, and I wake with a feeling of disorientation like I don't belong. I have a crazy headache. The pounding in my head won't stop. A bitter taste glosses my lips, and my mouth is dry. I feel like I've been wrestling in my sleep, and I'm exhausted. I begin to ask myself, *how is it possible to sleep for almost six hours and feel as tired as I do?* I should be well rested, but I'm still tired. I know I have to get up, the kids should be home soon. It's 2:00 p.m. and the kids come home from school at 2:30. One step from the bed and I know something is wrong, because I'm in pain. My leg hurts. The inner part of my thighs hurt, as well as my arms. As I make my way to the bathroom, I search my thoughts for an answer as to what could be the problem. I begin to remember like it was a dream that someone was punching me (Now I know, at this moment as I live and breathe, he was trying to inflict pain on me on purpose). Nothing made any sense, and because I couldn't explain it, I brushed it off.

    The next day, I had a bruise on the inner part of my thigh. It was a medium-sized black and blue mark about the size of a matchbox car. Not big, but large enough for me to notice. I began to think, *what on earth did I do last night or even the night before?* I hadn't fallen or slammed into anything, which wasn't uncommon for me, but I knew I hadn't hurt myself at work. There were times when I had been a little clumsy and careless, but not as of lately.

My job was pretty physical. At the time of this incident, I was working for the phone company. I had been there for 15 short years. That's where I met Craig. He was a technician. I walked into the office, and there he was. Craig wasn't a tall man. He stood about 5ft 8" and had a medium skin tone. He wasn't light-skinned or dark-skinned. His complexion reminded me of a Hershey chocolate bar. He was somewhere in the middle. He wore glasses and had a teddy bear build. Not fat, just a little thick. My job at that time was to go into customers' homes and fix their phones. Just like Craig, I was also a field technician. It was a much simpler job than my current one. When your phone stopped working, for whatever the reason, I was the technician that was dispatched to fix it. Currently, I work in the Line Gang. To say my job is pretty physical is an understatement. The work can be, and is, very strenuous on most days. As a lineman, I spend most of my time underground. Some of the manhole covers weigh more than I do. As a matter of fact, I'm sure they all weigh more than I do. Coming in at the height of 5ft 2" and 125 lbs., I am a small person, and as a lineman, my duties include replacing phone cables and fiber cables. All of which require me to venture into a world known to most as where the Teenage Mutant Ninja Turtles live—underground. People get a kick out of me when I try to explain my job to them. Essentially, we are also responsible for removing cables that are no longer working properly. These copper cables as they fail slowly, make way for future, more reliable fiber optic cables which we install and remove as well. When I tell people that I work in manholes underground, they always look at me with a smile and say, "Wow, I never would have guessed that." Truth be told, neither would I, but I love my job. However, on this particular day at work, I could not remember injuring myself on anything in the hole or even falling. So you can imagine my surprise when I noticed the bruise on my leg and felt the pain.

I'm in the bathroom staring at my leg wondering, *Where on earth...what on earth happened?*

More bruises showed up over the week, and Craig started pointing them out to me. This was very disturbing to me because he knew where the bruises were. He made sure to bring them to my attention. I'm left wondering now, was it to gloat because he knew what was happening, or to try and remove himself from the equation? As of late, I had a habit of showering and getting completely dressed in the bathroom so I wouldn't provoke him in any way. I mean, completely dressed down to my sneakers and socks I'd come out of the bathroom. I deluded to presume *out of sight, out of mind,* and it was my goal to stay out of his sight so I could stay out of his mind. I didn't want him to ask me for sex.

I can recall one evening as I was getting ready for work.

TAP...TAP...TAP

"Yes," I responded reluctantly.

We had just finished dinner, and I was rushing to get ready for work. I worked during the night hours. It afforded me the opportunity to be at home when my children got home from school.

"Can I come in? I need to get something from under the sink," he asked.

I was a little annoyed because I didn't want to be late. I quickly covered myself up with the towel.

"Ok, come in," I said.

As I stepped out of the shower with the towel wrapped around me, he said to me, "Your man needs to be more careful, he's starting to leave marks." Then he started to laugh. I looked at him and said, "WHAT?" I was getting so tired of all the comments that he was making. We weren't on the best of speaking terms. The marriage, our marriage, was over. We had become roommates. We were living the illusion of happiness, love, and bliss. Imagine waving to your significant other as they leave for work, all while thinking to thank God—I finally have time to myself. Sadly, that had become our reality.

He grabbed my shoulders, took me to the mirror and then turned me around, showing me this black and blue mark on my back.

Fear and panic rushed through my entire body. All I wanted to do was cry. How in the world did he know it was even there? I didn't realize it was there, and I was never naked around him. Questions immediately started coming to mind. Being that my routine was to get completely dressed in the bathroom because I didn't want to get him all riled up in any way, I was confused. We weren't having sex, so imagine my immediate concern. I'm almost certain in his mind that he thought I was, but I wasn't having sex with anyone. I intended to stay covered up at all times. Again, I didn't want him to look anywhere in my direction and ask to have sex. When he came into the bathroom to get whatever he needed, I made sure I was covered, and I'm confident that I didn't turn around. So how could he have known that this bruise was there?

The dreams continued for a little while longer. Along with the dreams came lethargy and lightheadedness. I was dizzy most of the time. I had no coordination. I kept dropping things at work, and my coworkers started to call me, "High Risk." During this time, it felt like I was going the distance with someone. I was fighting for my life.

I remember shaking uncontrollably. It felt like I was getting sick, but I had no fever. I felt groggy, and I was out of breath most of the time while I slept. Almost as if I had stopped breathing a couple of times. Hands were around my throat cutting off my air supply just for a little while, then a release — then again no air, and again and again until he got tired.

In my "dreams" I remember "him" asking me questions. He asked loads and loads of questions.

Who is this person?

Are you sleeping with him?

What is the nature of your relationship?

Are you going to move?

Where do you want to live?

So many questions. Falling, falling so fast like Alice down the rabbit hole, this all felt like a dream. However, I knew better. I knew the truth. This was no dream. I was being drugged. I don't know what was used. I don't know how much was used. I can only remember bits and pieces. I want to remember it all so bad. Except, at what price would I pay? Will I be tormented by these thoughts for the rest of my life? I had not wanted this pain, but it seems that it found me, tapped me on the shoulder, and caressed parts of me that I had not been aware of. The pain slowly crept into every part of my body, and more questions quickly came to mind, "How did this happen?"

    I had a habit of having a glass of red wine every night with dinner. I had read that wine was healthy for you. So that's what I started to do. In an article written by Carissa Stanz, having one glass of wine a day has many health properties. A 5-ounce glass of wine contains antioxidants which in turn can attack free radicals that cause health problems. It can also boost your immune system by chasing off infections. Red wine contains phenols, which acts as a natural blood thinner, similar to the effects of aspirin. It sounded good to me because high blood pressure runs in my family. It can lower cholesterol, reduce the risk of type 2 diabetes, and also reduce the risk of cancer. So naturally, I thought why not just have one glass of wine a day with dinner. I've always wanted to remain on the healthy side, and since I had read about the health properties, there was no guilt in it.

Except I noticed that I was always tired after drinking my one glass of wine. Not just a regular tired. It felt as if I hadn't gotten any sleep all day. So after showering, I'd lay down for a couple of minutes so I wouldn't be as tired, before I made the hour-long journey to work. It never dawned on me to connect the dots to the wine until I got to the end of the bottle. Out poured a layer of what looked like a pinkish-white substance that hadn't fully dissolved. At the bottom of the Kendall Jackson bottle was the evidence that caused my lethargy and gave him the wings to "make me tell the truth" as he so conveniently put it. His voice echoes in my mind…

"You know I have ways of making you tell the truth," he said.

"Ok whatever," I shrugged him off. I had no idea what he was talking about, and I didn't even care to ask him. Something was on his mind, and it was well with my soul that he had figured it out on his own.

The pieces of the puzzle finally started coming together for me when he put this all on Facebook. One of his posts read,

Got that squirrel feeling again today. My need for a nut just keeps getting stronger. Think I'm going to wear a mask today. Secret squirrel to the rescue. Lol.

I'm angry because he had the nerve to put it on Facebook and laugh about what he was going to do. There was a couple more posts that followed during the next couple of days.

When life knocks u down, be sure to get up quickly. Someone is behind you.

Took a punch in the stomach today, feel enlightened!!! But it did hurt. What doesn't kill u makes u stronger. Lol!!!

This last post I believe was about me going to the doctor. Craig happened to go with me. It was for my yearly pap test. When the doctor asked me if I was having any problems, I told him that it hurt to sit. I knew something was wrong, but I didn't know what it was. The doctor checked me out and said everything was fine. The last post stayed with me; I couldn't let it go or put it out of my mind. I had to ask him what he meant by his latest post. When I asked, he explained that it was about one of his military buddies that was going through something.

I asked him again about a week later just to see what he would say, and he told me something different; I no longer trusted anything he told me. Changing the subject, he proceeded to tell me a story of how he defended his sister's honor. He had recently gone to his sister's house at night with a couple of his military buddies, all of whom had black masks on. They beat up her boyfriend. He said they beat him up so bad that they broke his jaw and put him in the hospital. He laughed and said, "He'll never put his hands on her again." As I stood there and looked at him in utter disbelief, I asked him how it was that he was so sure. For as long as I've known her, she has been with men who abuse her. Craig told me that she said she didn't feel loved unless her man was beating on her. He shrugged his shoulders, looked around as if we were being watched, and said he'd just have to go and do it again.

"Again?" I ask. "Your sister is going to have you in a jail cell somewhere."

"Oh well, that's my sister, and I'll do anything for her," he said.

"Yes I understand, because I too would do anything for my sister, but the best thing to do for her is get her some professional help instead of beating up every boyfriend that she has who she allows to beat on her."

The conversation continued a little further, but I don't think it even mattered. I stopped listening. What was done was done, and it didn't seem like Craig even cared to hear what I was saying to him. He thought that he was protecting her honor. I tried to explain to him that he's not going to be able to defend her if he isn't with her all the time. In addition to that, what makes him so sure this man will stop beating on her? The man who she was currently dating didn't even know that it was Craig, because he busted through the man's front door wearing a ski mask. No one knew it was him and his military buddies; not even his sister.

And now my life is changed, and I start falling faster down the hole. He was changing, and I question if I even knew who he was at all.

Unlike Alice and her new peculiar world with mysterious creatures that can talk and have great adventures, my wonderland is a land of pain, tears, and destruction. Mountains move, an earthquakes come, followed by a tornado. A tsunami of tears swell up seconds later, and it feels as if my life is over. Things are different, drastically different than the moment we met. Life was much simpler back then, but now this...this.

Not seeing clear images, I can remember having the conversations. I can remember having sex against my will, and I remember Craig asking me if it hurt. And when I told him "no" it made him mad, and he decided to be more forceful.

There was a time when I went to work and I used the bathroom before going out to the field, and looking down I noticed that my underwear was on backwards. Now I know there was a slight possibility that I put them on backward, but that's not what happened. There was no need for me to rush and make this type of careless mistake.

Because of the drugs, there was nothing I could do. I felt so out of control and weak. There was no way for me to fight back. There was no way for me to get away. I was a puppet on a string, and my puppet master was some sick, cruel human being who decided this was the best way to get sex and answers. He never thought I was going to remember. Of course, I can only speculate as to what was going on in his mind at that time, but I believe he felt that the drugs he had given me would keep me unaware of his psychotic plan. Desperate to have what he needed, like every murderer believing that they leave no clues, I'm sure he thought his method was foolproof. I don't know if Craig did this to someone before me, or if I was his first victim; however, I do remember it, even in bits and pieces.

Thinking back to a recent conversation, he informed me of a time when he went away on one of his two-week training events with his military brothers, and one of his friends complained that he woke up and "his ass was hurting". As he told me this, he laughed. Like this was a joke. I asked him if he was serious and he shrugged it off and said, "I don't know, but oh well."

At first, I thought he was joking, but now I know he was more than serious. Apprehension coated my stomach and wouldn't go away; I began to fall faster down the rabbit hole. I know now that it's all true. I wanted to scream at the top of my lungs. I was terrified as panic had my insides in knots.

I have been violated. I've been raped over and over and over again, and the world that I know of, the world that was calm, has come to an end. I don't want to take one more step, in any direction. I'm stuck, and I feel like my life is over.

"How in the world did this happen to me?" I ask myself.

"Why did this happen to me?"

"Why Lord, why me?"

"Why did you let this happen to me?"

These are the very thoughts that invade my mind.

At first, I didn't want to believe that my husband would do something like this to me. I told myself that he would never do something LIKE THIS. For me, this was borderline psychopathic behavior. I know there are crazy people in this world, but I considered myself to be a pretty good judge of character. Wrong!! As I begin to rationalize to help myself cope, I tell myself that I need some proof to shut out the doubt in my mind. So I rush to get dressed and go to the Rite Aid down the block to pick up a drug test. I needed to know. I needed to know and prove that my husband would never do THIS. I run down my front steps to my car, jump in, and think, *which way should I go?* But then it comes to me. Slowly I pull out the driveway, and among the hustle and bustle of our little town, I turn on Mandeville Street. The Chinese buffet that I've always wanted to go to suddenly doesn't even look the least bit appealing. The Shoprite follows next, and I begin to wonder if what I'm looking for is in the Supermarket. No, there would be too many people watching and looking at me. In my mind, that's all I can think about. The Rite Aid would do just fine.

I come to the traffic light and make a left turn into the parking lot. My body feels so heavy, almost as if I had become one with the car. I couldn't move for a second. I have to get out of the car. "One step at a time," I tell myself. I rush over to where the drug test kits were and pick up the test that I assume will test for everything. I snatch up the First Check Home Drug Test Kit, because this particular kit tests for 12 different types of drugs: Marijuana, Cocaine, Opiates, Meth, and Oxycodone just to name a few. I didn't know what was being used and I needed to find out. I go to the cashier and instantly feel shame and guilt because in my mind I think she knows. She knows what happened to me. She flashes a smile. "$12.35," she says. She takes my money and says, "Have a nice day." I know she's not involved in this craziness, but I'm cold and rude to her because I'm scared this is all true; then it's back to my car.

In the car on the way home I'm nervous, and my stomach is doing its usual flips again. I feel like I'm walking in a fog and my life is in slow motion. I pull into the driveway, put the car in park, and rush up the three flights of stairs to my master bathroom. Craig hadn't gotten home yet. He was at work, I think. Truthfully, I didn't know, nor did I even care.

When I tell you things were terrible, I mean really bad. I read the directions and started. Urinating in the cup lasted a lifetime.

Life stopped moving, and for the few short minutes it took to get my results, the world stopped spinning. This couldn't be happening to me, I kept telling myself over and over again.

"This isn't happening."

Tears start rolling down my face, a sweet release, and I begin to cry harder. It's probably a good thing because I was holding my breath. Maybe I can pass out and hit my head on the tub. It would be an honest accident, and then the result wouldn't even matter. I'm more scared than anything because that would mean I'm not a good judge of character. As a matter of fact, I'm a very poor judge of character if this test comes back HOT.

I waited the required 5 minutes that the test instructed before I read the results.

There are six rows, each with two chemicals abbreviated with three letters. According to the directions, if a line does not show up in that particular row, it means you test positive. As the lines start showing up in pink, I can't stop crying.

Oxy.....POSITIVE

Thc…..POSITIVE

TCA….POSITIVE

Maybe I'm not reading this right, I tell myself. So I recheck the directions and I try to make sense of all of this. Paranoia starts to set in. I need to go back and get another test because maybe this one is broken. Perhaps I did it wrong.

This can't be right.

Something is wrong.

I begin to rationalize. My mind seems to start playing tricks on me, and I keep telling myself this can't be happening. This isn't my reality. It can't be. Deep down inside, I don't want it to be. I just want to be normal. I wish for that normal life. All I could think was *Anything was normal, except this*. Except, that is not what's going on. I feel so sick inside. Nausea seems to come creeping up from my toes. My legs are weak, and I need to find someplace to sit, quickly. The bed was too far away, and in seconds I find myself on the floor.

It's terrifying that right away it was my first instinct to protect him and not myself. Maybe the nurturer in me jumped into protective mode, but I began to defend the wrong person—until I decided to test my urine again.

I wanted so much to make sense of everything that was happening to me. For me, there was only one thing to do. Of course, I had to go to my source—God. The All-knowing and the All-powerful. He is omnipresent. He is everywhere at all times. So for me, it meant that God saw this and knew that this was going to happen to me. There were so many more questions that crept into my mind, and I started to feel entitled to the answers.

Oh, how I prayed, "Lord, You are my rock. You are my comforter, and I don't feel comforted. Dejected from the discovery of this fresh new epiphany, I feel like you have abandoned me. You let him do this to me, and when I call out to You, You're nowhere to be found."

My heart is so heavy, and my mind is so cloudy right now. One minute I'm angry with God, and the next, I feel peace. YES! Angry is such a strong word, but it's how I feel. The rage inside of me is at a melting point, and my insides cry out for justice. A man who I once loved has violated me and then decided to brag about it on Facebook.

What doesn't kill you makes you stronger, he posts.

I must have read those words over and over about a thousand times. Indignation and resentment begins to fester in me, and the only thing that comes to mind is one word..."WHY?"

I have always thought of myself as a good person. I try my best to help anyone that I can. It's tough for me to see a person in need and just walk away and not do anything. It's the right thing to do. Too many times, I've heard people tell me that I'm too nice. It didn't matter, because I've always figured it would come back to me one way or another. Even if it didn't, I know they needed it. I never did any of it because I wanted something in return. I've always helped because it was the right thing to do.

The Bible reads, "The strong bear the infirmities of the weak" (Romans 15:1) and I stood on His Word.

Never have I professed that I was perfect because no one in this world is. But I do believe that we are supposed to try every day to be better than we were yesterday. Each day my eyes opened, I believed it was another chance for me to get it right. And each day was just that - another chance for me.

I can't piece together these new chains of events to come to some conclusion as to why this has happened to me. I needed answers. I had so many questions. I have so much anger inside me now. I'm angry at Craig, of course, but I'm also mad at God.

Thinking back on my life now, before the rape, it wasn't always so complicated. However, I realized I couldn't go back. I can't erase what has happened to me, no matter how much I'd like to. I have to put one foot in front of the other and move forward, but I honestly don't know how. All I feel is the pain.

Chapter 2

The Dream

Craig was always an easy person to talk to. Moreover, I've always thought of him to be very wise because he always gave out great advice. Funny thing, the world must have known it, too. When we were out and about, whether to the supermarket or the mall, so many people would come up to him and tell him their life story. He'd always sit there and listen, and somehow come up with a solution to their life problems. Most of his advice came in handy, too. It felt good being around him. At the beginning of our relationship, I remember sitting back and talking for hours about nothing and everything—long conversations about life. Conversations we never wanted to hang the phone up from because our expression of view kept us entwined and stimulated. We'd dip into each other's past, and it was nice getting to know him. We talked about the past, about how it shaped and molded us into the fearless rebels we were at that exact moment. He was a rebellious child, and at the age of 16 decided to leave his mother's house when she demanded money for electricity. He laughed, "My mother wanted me to pay her electricity bill." His tone was sharp and cold. You seem to be like every teenager growing up in our mother's house; we think we know everything. We know when to come and when to go as we please, of course. We even know when it is time to get a job. And it was mainly time for him to involve himself in the particular fact of life...finding a job. It was easy for him to find a job because he was a hustler. No matter what the situation was, he was going to work it and get paid. Sell ice to an Eskimo? No problem, he was on it. He had it covered.

He was a very articulate man. Getting what he wanted came easily to him like it was second nature. He didn't even have to think about it. What he had was a natural gift that none other than GOD Himself gave to him, because he was so good at it. Sometimes I'd stand amazed at how he was able to talk to the customers at work. This one particular time, he messed up a customer's wall installing their new phone line. They had some special paint just painted on the wall a couple of days earlier. After a few minutes, the customer decided not to put in a claim, but instead redo the paint themselves. These encounters were just an everyday thing with him. Like a moth to a flame, little did I know I'd be burned by his fire.

Things with him, in the beginning, were a little shaky. And yet again, I brushed it off because I believed that we were in the beginning stage of our relationship, and it wasn't going to be perfect. He told me that he wasn't seeing anyone and he'd just gotten out of a relationship because his girlfriend cheated on him. Quickly I felt sorry for him and took his side. I didn't even question him as to the actions that led up to their falling out. I just assumed that she was crazy for leaving such a great guy. I counted myself blessed and lucky all at the same time.

In the beginning, we had to keep our relationship hush hush because we worked together. We decided that we would keep it quiet until we saw where it was going.

I, just recently separated, didn't see the need to rush into anything fast, but I really couldn't help myself - maybe because I wanted it. I wanted Craig and what he had to offer. I wanted my children to see what he had to offer. When we met, Justin was eight years old, Gabriel was 6, and Melissa was 4. They seemed to get along really well. He'd play with them, and we would do what normal parents did. I thought to myself, WOW this is cool. Things are going so well. It's not every day that you find a man who loves you and even loves and wants to help you take care of kids who aren't also his. Yes, Lord, I had been blessed, or so I thought.

By all means, I'm not insinuating that everything was perfect, but things were genuinely good. I had nothing to complain about. Like every couple, we had our little spats, but the honeymoon was still on and popping. We were still one, and we felt comfortable to take our relationship to the next level.

Now after a couple of months, we threw caution to the wind and slowly invited the world into our relationship. I started going over to Craig's house more and more, and spending the night was always an option. It had now been our routine. If I didn't have the kids, I was spending time with him. It was just Craig and me. Plans to live together became another topic of our everyday discussions right along with what was for dinner. There was no need to rush things, because he had a two bedroom apartment in the Bronx. So we were comfortable, until I got pregnant.

Now it was time to kick things into high gear and look for a place of our own. We didn't know if it would be an apartment or a house, but the search was on. Would we stay in the city or maybe find an apartment in the Bronx where we already lived? I didn't feel the need to get anything significant, just a little something. A three-bedroom apartment would have been more than enough, I assumed, and now that a baby was coming, we could keep him or her in the room with us. Stash a little cash and possibly get an even bigger house a little later down the road.

    During the search, the unthinkable happened. Two planes flew into the World Trade Center, and the world was at war. I remember exactly where I was that day. I had just gotten to work. I worked on 47th Street and 11th Avenue at the time. It was conveniently right off the West Side Highway, not even a block away. It was nestled between 11th Avenue and the West Side Highway right next to the famous Intrepid Museum. The other garage I had worked at was on the east side of town. This new location was a lot more accessible. During the morning rush hour, just as the sun started to kiss the sky as some of us had just walked inside our garage, someone came running in, shouting,

    "THERE'S SMOKE, A LOT OF SMOKE COMING FROM DOWNTOWN"

Everyone ran out the building to check out the enormous amount of smoke coming from the location that was unknown to us, except the direction—downtown. I then ran back in the building, and it was all over the news. My first thought was that I needed to get to my kids. So I called the school and told them I was on my way. I told my boss that I was taking the rest of the day off. Not knowing exactly what was going on, fear was the only thing I could process. Immensely scared, because I didn't know what was going to happen next.

"Is there something going to happen, or do you think that was it?" I asked my co-worker who was leaving with me.

"I don't know," he said, "But I'm getting the hell up out of here before something does."

Suddenly, staying in the Bronx was no longer an option for us. If there were going to be any more terrorist attacks, or whatever was about to start happening, I thought it best to remove the children from any harm that possibly might come our way. So now the decision was even easier, "It was time to get out of Dodge."

Our search resulted in a small cute little townhouse community about an hour away from work, in Warwick, New York, with other cute families that had children of their own. Warwick was known for its Applefest and rolling farmlands. When we first had a chance to visit, all I could think about when I saw it was, "Oh honey look, friends, the kids will have lots and lots of friends." I was in love. The schools were perfect, unlike the city with their overcrowded classrooms our kids had become accustomed to. It was a new world for us, and I was so glad to be a part of it with my "littles". As a parent, I wanted to make sure that they would be safe and have the opportunity to thrive. Not only that, but I needed peace of mind. Inevitably things happen all over the world, yes, but I didn't want us to be in the heart of the craziness, the mayhem, and destruction if anything started to jump off. This was it for me. We made an offer on the house, and it was ours. Easy enough process; I sincerely wondered what all the people were talking about. The home buying process happened so quickly, and we didn't have any issues. So naturally, I believed it was fate. God had led us to the promised land.

    The commute took some time getting used to, but after a year or so I could get to work and back without dozing off. I even contemplated asking one of the guys at work if he'd like to commute with me, but that conversation never came up because I decided to drive on my own. In the beginning, it was rough. I remember a rest stop that was somewhat in the middle of my commute. I had to pull over several times and take a nap. The Sandman always crept up on me right before I'd get to that particular spot. As if it was already ingrained in my DNA that I'd reached the spot and it was time for my body to completely shut down. Fearful that I might cause an accident, I gladly accepted the invitation from my premature acquaintance and pulled over for some rest. "Just for a little while," I'd tell myself, "so I can make it home."

My power nap afforded me the necessary courage and fortitude to continue the rest of my trip. Thirty minutes may not seem like much, but when I was exhausted, it seemed like time stood still no matter how many miles I drove. I can honestly say I take my hat off to the truck drivers, Uber drivers, or any drivers for that matter. The driving profession isn't easy. No matter how short the drive, I can jump in the car and it slowly soothes me to sleep. I swear, the Sandman is always riding shotgun, except he's not helping me watch for any police, nor is he talking me to any of my destinations. I would have kicked him to the curb, but I needed him in my life.

Day by day, we began to build with each other and grow more like one. Each day was another day to learn something new about each other and it felt good. We laughed, we cried, and fought about little things, stupid things, and important things. I recall one of our fights had me thinking whether I was moving a little too fast. This great offense, for me anyway, was his selective amnesia. He forgot to tell me that he offered a ride to his co-worker who didn't live too far from us. Each morning he would leave the house and pick her up, and they would drive to work. I would have been a little more understanding if we could have at least talked about it before he had offered her a ride. Maybe I would have also been a bit more understanding if she drove. However, no, she never drove; he was always the designated driver. So naturally, I had to voice my opinion when I found out that this had been going on for about a month. His excuse, "I didn't think you'd mind; it was completely harmless." Now, I've never been the jealous type, but something about this didn't sit right with me. If it was as harmless as he claimed, why didn't he tell me about it? I don't know, maybe I was going crazy, or maybe there was something that was indeed there. However, I was not willing to invest any more brain power on this subject, so I just put it to the back of my mind and forgot about it.

Over the next couple of months, the kids settled into their new neighborhood, and things were going well. The kids were especially glad that they were able to take the bus to school in the morning. It tickled me because they would get up so early, get dressed, and make sure they were completely ready so they wouldn't miss the bus. It wasn't because they wanted to get to school on time. It was only because they didn't want to miss the bus. When we were in the city, I had to take them to school every morning, and they would always say they wished they could ride the bus to school like the other kids. Unfortunately, we lived too far away for the bus, so I had to take them to school.

Craig and I were enjoying our new home as well. Even though we worked different shifts, we still made time for each other. It was hard, but I knew it had to be done if we wanted to keep the spark going. So we decided to have date night on Fridays. Contributing to our happiness was easy. It was where I wanted to be. And when you're happy, everything comes easy. It didn't matter if we went out or stayed inside; whether we had dinner and drinks or a walk in the park. I was just happy being by his side. And he was happy being by mine.

Things were going well. Craig had applied for a new management position at our job which afforded us a little more money. Not necessarily more time, but a bit more money. Then before I could finish hanging the pictures and sending out the invitations to the housewarming, Craig came in the house and said he lost his job.

"Excuse me?" I thought I was hearing him wrong. "Say that again."

"I think I'm getting fired!" he says.

"But why?"

"For closing out jobs the wrong way," he says. He's vexed, and I can hear it as he speaks.

He said that he was given specific instructions to close out his jobs a certain way by his manager after he finished seeing a customer, but corporate security said it was fraud. I was instantly relieved because I thought it was an easy fix.

"Ok, so go back and tell Corporate what you just told me."

"I did," he said, "but it's his word against mine, and he's not going to incriminate himself if he knows now what he was telling me to do was wrong."

And just like that, he was fired. His manager's word against his and he was the one who got the boot.

Instantly, I tried to restore what was broken. I explained to Craig that we were going to be okay. Things would be ok. There was nothing to worry about, and we were in this together. His next statement was, "I don't feel like a man if I'm not making more money than you."

"Listen, Craig, I know that if I lost my job, you got me...right"?

"Of course."

"Then why would you assume any different of me? I love you, and I got you!"

No matter how hard I tried to reassure him that things were going to be good, he sunk further and further into despair. Days and nights for him were spent watching TV. He didn't even want to get up and try to look for a job. I'd leave for work, and he would be lying across the bed; and when I came home, he'd be in the same spot. Date nights became a thing of the past because now I had to cover all the bills, and we needed every single penny.

As if we didn't have enough bad news for a year, one of Gabriel's teachers sent home a note saying he wasn't turning in his homework. Her note proceeded to tell me that Gabriel was a bright boy, no behavioral problems - just that he wasn't doing his homework. Now because I worked nights, I was upstairs asleep, and Craig was downstairs when

Gabriel came home with the note. Suddenly, Craig starts screaming at the top of his lungs, which woke me out of my sleep. I rushed downstairs because I thought something was wrong, someone was hurt, or something was terribly wrong. I was honestly not prepared for the catastrophe that was about to take place.

"Why didn't you do your homework?" Craig asks Gabriel

"I don't know," Gabriel says.

"Why didn't you do your homework?" he screams even louder.

"I don't know," Gabriel says again.

"I'm going to ask you one more time, and you better have an answer for me. Why didn't you do your homework?"

The next thing I knew Craig picked Gabriel up and started throwing him around the kitchen, slamming him into the wall and the refrigerator. He threw him across the table and picked him up again and threw him across the room. This time Gabriel landed by the fridge. He picked him up by his neck and then slammed his head into the corner of the wall, breaking the wall. He put my baby's head through the wall. I screamed and pleaded for him to stop. He dropped Gabriel to the floor; my boy was crying profusely while holding his head.

"I'm calling the police!" Gabriel cries. Craig says nothing.

I look at him and ask, "What is your problem, are you crazy, why would you do that to him?"

Again, Craig says nothing.

From that moment on, Craig wasn't the same Craig anymore. He was an evil, deranged crazy person that put my baby's head through the wall.

My mind was very uneasy, and just like that, in a matter of seconds there was no peace in my home, and our dream was no longer joyful, pleasant, loving, cheerful, intoxicating or carefree. In the blink of an eye it was tainted and polluted. The dream, our dream, of "Love racing fast at top speed suddenly crashing", and ultimately I was heartbroken. A short poem written by my best friend Brenda Henry, *And Now I See Him Down on His Knees*. Gabriel's tears can't wipe away any of this hurt. This grown man flexed his muscles and brought my 12-year-old on his knees.

"Why had I not seen this side of him before?" I began to ask myself.

"Had I seen this side of him and completely missed it?"

"Did I ignore all the red flags?"

"Were there any red flags?"

I don't even care anymore. Now I have to protect Gabriel. Two days or so goes by, and I tell him that I want a divorce. Did I discuss this with God? Absolutely not, but I felt sure that I wasn't going to be able to take another step further with Craig.

"Please don't," he says, "let's go to counseling first." Reluctantly, I agreed. It didn't matter to me because I was going to tell my side, and the counselor and God would understand, and I was cool with that. However, in the back of my mind, I was scared. How would I protect Gabriel and all the kids if I still had to go to work? So to put my mind at ease, I took the day off the next day and the day after that. I knew something had to be done because there was no way I was going to be able to take the rest of the month off, too. Here we are at the beginning of September, and I know I don't have a whole school year worth of days off.

We take the long journey to see the counselor who happens to be married to a friend of mine. He's the pastor of the church we go to. The stress of what has transpired forces me to replay the events over in my mind once more. Craig tries to make small talk and I am unwilling to hold any conversation as we travel because that would mean engaging in what I believe to be useless and a waste of my time; so we travel to the session in silence. My mind has already been made up.

We travel for about an hour or so to the church. We had a 9:00 a.m. appointment, and I didn't want to be late. In my mind, I just wanted to hurry up and get over with it. Traveling to the church seemed like forever. I was mulling over in my mind exactly what I was going to tell the pastor. I had a play-by-play of my presentation going on in my mind. If I could have made a PowerPoint presentation, I would have. I intended to make sure the pastor knew precisely how I felt because I wanted his blessing to run for the hills. We get off the highway and make a quick left. Drive two blocks past the Pizza Hut and make another left. The church wasn't particularly far from the road, but it was a little bit off a ways. About 10 minutes later we pull up to the church, and my insides get tight again. I'm scared, happy, sad, and relieved all at the same time.

"Hello," he says. 'How's it going?" The pastor happened to be outside when we pulled into the parking lot, trying his best to make small talk. I know he can see on my face the disdain and reluctance of being there for this parley.

Not wanting to be rude, and also because this was the pastor, I utter one of the worst and deadliest terms women use today, "I'm fine." As I usher those words into existence, all I want to do is scream.

We climb the small flight of four steps that lead into the church. My mind is drawn to a much happier place and I don't want to be at church. I want to tell the pastor what happened and get back home to my kids. In my mind, I've already seen how this conversation should go. He explains his actions, I offer my insight into the abuse, the pastor agrees with me, and I can then go ahead with the divorce and keep it moving.

Up a large narrow hallway, we climbed more stairs to an opening of four rooms. Two of them used for offices and the third one looked like a classroom. As the pastor ushers us to the classroom, I notice the clouds outside the large picture window. They represent the melancholic delicacy of this situation. It has finally dawned on me that, had I not been there to stop this, my child could have died. The images play over in my head, but the one image that is on constant repeat is when he put Gabriel's head through the wall. The corner of the wall. He dented the metal bracket and put a hole in the wall.

"So tell me what's going on," the pastor interjects and brings me back to the present.

"He put Gabriel's head through the wall," I scream. I was livid. Anger swells up inside of me, and the rush of tears coming down my face fall as evidence of this pain. Craig's reply stunned me even more.

"Well, you know I had to show him who the boss was. I had to show him that I mean business," he said. "You know how little boys can get, and he needed to find out, unfortunately, the hard way that I mean what I say."

"So why couldn't you just spank him?" I ask.

"That wasn't going to do anything."

"How do you know if you didn't even try?"

"I want a divorce!" I cry out as the tears flow from my eyes even more. "This can never happen again."

"All right, that's enough. I need to speak to the both of you separately," the pastor intercedes, quickly shutting the door on our argument.

I go outside and into one of the adjourning offices to the classroom. All sorts of books line the wall in a large wooden bookcase, and I wish I could take one to hide away in from this grievously dark chapter of my life. After what seemed like forever, but in actuality was only about 15 minutes that I was standing there reading which books seemed interesting, and on the verge of walking out with my mind all made up, the pastor sticks his head out and says, "Can you come in, please?" He exhales a long sigh. It almost sounds as if he was sorry for me. "Now I'd like to talk with you." I know these type of counseling sessions were hard on him. "Have a seat. Tell me what happened." My heart sinks. It feels as if it jumped into the pit of my stomach and yet again I had to relive the entire distress of watching my son's head be put through a wall. I wanted so much to go back and have that out-of-body experience where I could predict the future and see the events before they unfold, so I can somehow save my son from the damage and harm that would soon shake loose the bond and crumble the foundation of safety that I was able to provide him. A divide was on its way unbeknownst to me, and there wasn't anything I could do to stop it.

As the pastor and I sat and talked for what seemed like a couple of forevers, I unloaded all my anger and frustration on him, and I was furious. Gabriel was my child, and somehow I failed him. How could I let this happen? Did I miss a sign somewhere? How could this little boy have provoked this? He was twelve years old. Again, trying to rationalize and make sense of this adversary that crept into our home uninvited, I truly didn't want to believe he would do something like this. As we continue the conversation, I try to hold back my tears because I don't want to cry, but I can't seem to help it. The rush of tears swell up inside of me as if Craig had just dug a well. The more they come, the more I try to stop them, but I can't. They won't stop. "I want a divorce!" I tell the pastor. Firmly, I state my intentions. "I'm not sure that is a good thing to do," he replied. His response floors me.

"Let's do a couple more counseling sessions first and see how you feel later. I know you're angry and sometimes when we are angry, we make rash decisions that we later regret." With his hands folded in front of him and a concerned look on his face, I see he really wants me to think over what seems to be my premature and impulsive decision. With my mouth I said, "Ok," but with my heart, I said, "There's no way I'm going to let this happen again." I was determined to be at every place and time so that I could keep all the kids safe. Impossible? Maybe, but until I could convince the pastor that this was the best decision for me, I had to split myself in two, three, or fours if necessary.

Craig turns to the pastor and says thank you, and I'm left confused as to where I went wrong in our dialogue. Did he not hear me? Did he not understand what I explained to him? What just happened? Was there some male bonding when I left the room? I just wanted to stop thinking so bad.

These were all the questions and more I began to work over and over in my mind on the way home from my talk with God's chosen one. Frustration and Anger were my new best friends.

As the day turned into night, in the blink of an eye, I disconnected. Craig was no longer mine. It didn't matter what the pastor said. He was no longer my husband. He hurt me by damaging my son.

My commute to work caused me so much anxiety. The jobs at work now cause me anxiety as well. All I kept thinking about was that at any minute the same thing could be happening all over again. So many different scenarios played over and over in my head, and I felt helpless. How was I supposed to protect them while I was away from them at work? Craig was no longer the protector. In a matter of minutes, he had become the enemy, and our family was broken. The only release came as I was driving home because I knew I'd soon be back with my babies.

Chapter 3

Break it Down

Anxiety, another new best friend of mine, whispered and told me that this was going to happen again, and doubt crept up on me and caught me off guard. How was I supposed to protect them? I felt like a complete failure for not being able to defend him. I couldn't breathe. I didn't want to breathe, and what made it worse was that I was now assuming responsibility for this action because I brought the fight to my son's door. To say I was hard on myself was an understatement. I was more than angry with everything that was going on and was equally saddened because I had no resolution. I knew what I wanted to do, but no one gave me their blessing. Not even God Himself, and I felt trapped. Trapped because the pastor said I had to stay. I was stuck because my friends also advised me to stay.

Trapped because I thought the whole world wasn't listening to me. I felt like standing on the top of the Empire State Building and saying, "Don't you people see what's going on?" I also felt like Craig used his God-given gift of gab to lull the pastor to sleep so that he could have an opportunity to do this again.

My home used to be a tranquil place. A place of peace. It used to be a place that I loved to be. The nightlife meant nothing to me. You could have all of that. I had my share of nights out, and it was no longer a necessity to see what all the fuss was about because now I knew and it wasn't anything to write home about. Now don't get me wrong, we had some great times, but I much rather stay at home with my family. Only now, his actions caused our home to be transformed into this place that caused great stress from the moment I walked through the door. My insides now always felt tight, and every breath that I breathed was shallow, almost as if I was purposely trying to suffocate myself.

Moreover, each step sent shockwaves throughout my body, a reminder of the day's events that would not go away. I didn't want to be home anymore, and it was pretty clear. Our house was no longer a home. As quickly as his actions changed the dynamics of our relationship, I willingly adapted. We would walk past each other and not say a word. What was the need? Things were uncomfortable, and I didn't care how he felt anymore. I was given a glimpse into the lives of the children who are being abused and women who are battered. I was given a spoon full of sensitivity. Indignantly, I baptized myself with an invisible shield because something like this should never, would never, or could never happen to me. This invisible shield of a perfect marriage or the ideal life maintained my false sense of protection and entitlement at that time. So now that this has happened, my foundation shaken once again, I'm unsure how to proceed with the rest of my life. Trembling inside, held captive by fear, I knew there was a decision that needed to be made. Would I or would I not continue with this marriage knowing that this could possibly happen again? What happens if it does? More questions attacked my consciousness, and I began to restore the hurt once again. These children were the gifts that God had given me, and it was my job to protect them NO MATTER WHAT! However, how was I supposed to do that married to someone who had abused them, and could abuse them again? For me, it was a no brainer. Protect the children. Protect the gifts that were given to me. Shame, guilt, fear, embarrassment, helplessness, and confusion were just a few of the emotions playing ping pong in my head. Each minute that passed felt like a lifetime, and I just wanted all the pain and hurt to stop. I wanted the world to stop turning for me. I wanted a moment to gather my thoughts and come up with an elaborate plan so I could quickly put it into action without wasting any more time in this crazy life of mine.

I began to pray; I needed an answer from God. My days turned into nights and then really long days. I waited for an answer. Back to work, I drove with the kids on my mind. I wondered if they were safe. At any moment, he could be throwing them all around the house again. Wondering if they could have made him angry and this time he had to do what he had to do again. That was the explanation he gave to the pastor.

"A MAN HAS TO DO WHAT A MAN HAS TO DO." Those were his exact words.

Pulling into the garage at work I looked at the clock, and my heart began the countdown. I could feel the ache. Seven and a half more hours before I get home to my littles.

Sinister

Sinister could always make me laugh. He had this way about himself. He was determined to have a good day. Something that I was no longer able to do. He was very funny, and we were always laughing and clowning. I would always look at him and shake my head. After just a few short weeks of getting to know him, I knew exactly how he was as a child, and I had no doubt in my mind that he was voted class clown.

And as I sit mulling over my recent events, and the damage that has me anxious day in and day out, I quickly begin to make a critical mistake. I started to laugh at his jokes.

Sinister was tall. 6'4" and about 220 pounds. Yes, Sinister is an unusual name, and no, his mother didn't name him that, but it was his nickname. One day I asked him how he acquired such an ominous name, and he said it was given to him because people say he had that look. I shake my head and say ok, it's your name, not mine.

I remember the first time we met. We were in the locker room, and it was just he and I. He started making small talk, and I asked him his name. He said, "My name is Sinister."

"You can't be serious, I know your mother didn't name you Sinister," I replied.

"No," he begins to laugh, "my name is Benjamin."

"Ok cool, I'll call you Benjamin then."

We talked a little while longer, but then duty called, and we had to go to work.

As the final hour approaches, a sigh of relief escapes, and I'm left thanking God that this man put a smile on my face and kept me grounded - even if it was just for a short while. Driving home, I begin praying and thanking God that I haven't gotten that phone call telling me one of my children is in the hospital and that he was very sorry once again.

"Sorry, but they left him no choice."

After an hour drive, I'm finally in my driveway, and all anxiety has melted away. I walk through the front door. Grateful, I climb the steps as quickly as I can, being careful not to wake the children. I check on them to make sure they are all ok. Upon each step, the photos on the wall remind me of their innocence. School pictures of the children when they were in kindergarten meet me as I climb the stairs which lead to my room. I take a long slow deep breath and softly whisper once again, "Thank You" as I stand in the doorway to the boy's room.

Craig is asleep, and I'm more than a little happy, to say the least, that I don't have to interact with him. His voice has now become that sound of fingernails scratching on a chalkboard. I don't want to hear it anymore. It vexes me. So I slip as quietly as I possibly can into the bathroom to take a shower. I pick up everything I need to come out fully dressed.

The water is set on fire, just the way I like it, and before I can enter the tub, I let the bathroom fill up with steam. I find it soothing to sit there, plus I read in an article of Men's Health that saunas can relieve stress. "Studies have shown improvement in symptoms of depression…and the ability to relax," says Dr. Sugar Shah, M.D. At that particular time, stress was all I knew. Among other things, saunas can protect the brain. It also can help your muscles recover faster after an intense workout in the gym. Patients with chronic pain can also benefit from the use of saunas, as well as lower your cholesterol. My little bathroom wasn't exactly a sauna, but I was going to fill it up with as much steam as possible and take it in for as long as I could. I just wanted to relax. A shower was next to wash all the cares away.

After my shower, I quickly get dressed so I can go to sleep. I was always so tired at this point. My thoughts were draining me. I was constantly being bombarded with, *did I do enough to protect my son*? Constant feelings of not being able to defend him slipped through the cracks of each thought. Knowing that I was not going to be able to be with him at all times. Did I do enough? Was I going to be enough? I intended to tiptoe out of the bathroom, but as soon as I opened the door, I saw that Craig was awake. Speaking was now a luxury that he could no longer afford. I walked past him and climbed right into bed. I wanted him to know that I meant business. I was angry and hurt, and I didn't want to give him any idea that what he did was acceptable. So I quickly climbed into bed and closed my eyes. Alone with my thoughts, I began praying. I wanted to thank God again for His Grace and His Mercy. My children were my everything. They were the very air that I breathed. Life would never be the same without every single one of them. I don't even think he understood that. I don't think he realized, at any particular moment while he was picking him up and throwing him around the kitchen that he could have ever taken that whole ordeal from me. It was viciously burned in my memory. With that being said, his only answer for his actions was, "I'm sorry." An interesting meme once read:

Grab a plate and throw it on the floor. Did it break? Yes? Ok, now tell it you're sorry. Good, now did it unbreak? Now you understand...exactly

The earth has opened up and there is no ground beneath me. I begin to fall. I feel like someone has snatched all the talk out of me. In mid-air, I stop, and now I'm in my bed. I can hear all the voices, and I want to cry out for help, but no one can hear me. I can't move. It's coming toward me. A figure that I have never seen before. Walking slowly, I know he is evil, I can feel it, and I'm scared. Finally, I realize that I'm dreaming, and as he comes closer I see that I must wake myself up. Soon he's on top of me looking at me. Slowly he brings his face toward mine; all the flesh is gone. Only skin and bones remain, and he just looks at me. All I can do is think, "Help Me." My father used to tell us children that if this ever happened, it was a witch who was riding your back. My lips are sealed shut. There is nothing I can do as we are now face to face. Then in a split second, I feel a sharp pain in my chest. The bed starts shaking. This is it; I'm going to die, I tell myself. I feel the vibration once again. My eyes open and I wake to a text message on my cell phone. I roll over and take a long deep breath. It felt so real and draining. I was never more thankful for a text message in my life. I look at my phone, but my eyes won't come into focus. I blink a few times, and my eyes adjust to the light and my surroundings. It's a text message from Sinister.

Hey, what's going on?

I look around for a second and then look back at my phone, "What time is it?" I search for the time on my cell phone. It's 2:12 in the afternoon. It wasn't uncommon for me to have his cell number. We all had each other's numbers. At work, we used two-way radios, and if the radios died, we would need another form of communication to talk with each other so that the work could still continue.

I was sleeping, but your text just woke me out of this crazy dream, I text.

Well, I guess you owe me one for saving your life, he texts back.

I laugh to myself, but I was honestly thankful that demon didn't get me.

"What's up," I text.

Do you have Ivy's number? I'm in her neighborhood, and I'd like to ask her if she would want to go out for a cup of coffee.

I laugh to myself, and quickly say no, even though I did have her number. I was not in the business of giving out any one's name and number unless they said it was ok. I text Ivy and ask if it's ok to give out her cell number and she says it's cool. Right before I text Sinister back, he texts me that he found her number. Ok, I reply and drift back into La La land, hoping that I don't drift back toward the same beast of the underworld that held me captive.

After another hour of sleep, I wake because I know the kids should be coming home soon. The sound of their voices when they come home gives me wings. It's time to get up; no more sleep until I come back tomorrow morning. I sit up and let my feet dangle over the edge of the bed.

It's 2:45 p.m. and I hear the front door open, and the heavy thumping of feet running up the steps. Then comes a light knock on the door. "Come in," I say.

"Hello Mommy," my oldest comes into the room. "Did you have a good nap?" he asks. Of course, I don't tell him about the witch that stole my words. I quickly tell him yes and ask him about his day. He begins to talk about everything he learned in each class, and it almost seems like he said it all without taking one single breath. I could tell the kids loved their new house and school, because every time they talked about anything they would light up and give me all the details. They loved to share all about their day.

Smiles quickly turned into frowns as Craig comes into the room. "What's for dinner?" he asks. I ignore him as if he isn't there. I look at my oldest boy. "Go to the kitchen table and start your homework. I'll be down in a minute." As soon as the boy leaves the room, I look at Craig as if to give him a look of "Don't even talk to me."

"Can we please talk?" he asks.

"No," I reply, "I have nothing to say to you."

"But I'm sorry for what happened."

"I don't care what he has to say. Craig was that piece of meat that had fallen on the floor. There was no 5-second rule here. He was never going to be the same. I wasn't about to pick him up and rinse him off. I was more than comfortable with throwing him in the trash. I was so frightened by his behavior that I didn't want to retake a chance of this happening, only now I'm haunted each day by the details. People go to jail for actions like those. I didn't want to have to spend the rest of my life behind bars by default, whether it be because I knew what was going on, or because I couldn't stop the madness. I didn't want any part of his actions. I didn't want to be responsible for the hurt that he expelled on my children.

"I need you to know that I am the least bit concerned with how sorry you are," I tell him once more.

I walked downstairs and prepared dinner. In my heart, I'm still not sure of how to handle this delicate situation. Craig's my husband, and it's *for better or for worse*, and somehow we have stumbled onto the *worse* so soon into our marriage. My life was extremely complicated, but be that as it may, something still had to be done. I begin to pray to God again for answers, and I tell myself again to wait for a reply.

After dinner, my stomach began to do its usual flips. It was time for me to leave the children once again and it broke my heart because I started thinking that this could be the last time that I saw them again. I had to go to work because I was the only one working, and I didn't have anyone to watch them at the time. This whole situation had me between a rock and a hard place. I was damned if I did, and damned if I didn't. Either way, I was in trouble.

I go warm the car up and immediately start praying, "Lord, please watch over my children. Please don't let him hurt them." I jump in the car, look back at the house in the rear view mirror and begin the commute to work with a heavy heart once again. Tonight I had to figure out how I was going to stay home with them longer. Finding out how many days I had left for the year was a priority.

Sinister was getting out of his car when I pulled into the garage. He waited until I got out of my car, and said, "Don't think I forgot that you owe me." I just took one look at him and started crying. Overwhelmed with the day's events and my anxiety, I couldn't mask the hurt any longer. Without even blinking, he put his arms around me and hugged me. He pulled me in close and just held me until I got myself together.

"He put my son's head through the wall."
"Who?"
"Craig!"
"Wait I don't understand, what happened?"

Not even wanting to relive these details, I begin to tell him what my mind won't let me forget.

The look on his face was of anger. He began to ask about Gabriel and how he was doing. Again, the tears started to slip from the vault. It was nice to have someone to talk to, and someone who was willing to listen.

"You know it's going to be all right. I know it seems bad right now, but it will be ok, and Gabriel will be ok also."

"I know, but I'm so scared that, at this very moment, anything could happen," I tell him.

"You can't think like that. Just pray, and let God do the rest," he says. The son of a preacher, Sinister knew who God was, and he believed. He believed that God was in control, and he was trying to encourage me of that. It was refreshing because my heart was so heavy at that exact moment. Sinister knew what I needed to hear, and for that short amount of time, my mind was renewed. I believed God would do what I had asked Him, which was to keep watch over my babies, but there was still some doubt.

Holding back from the night's task of work was no longer on my mind. It was much easier for me to complete the night's work without my mind being harassed by the past. A heavy burden had been lifted. Such a small drop of encouragement, but it was just what I needed at the right time. Now work could proceed as planned. Cultivating a moment that has been delivered by my friend and now feeling lighter, I could finally concentrate on paying the bills. Tonight's job was to remove cables along 2nd Avenue in Manhattan. It seems that the company either no longer needed, or were going to use these big 2400 copper cables and they needed to be removed. Entrusted with the task of making room for the new wave of the future—fiber optics and the new 2nd Avenue Subway Line—we rolled out the garage to set up at our selected location.

Driving these big outdated heavy trucks kept the lights on. Replacing and removing cables kept food on the table, and staying out of harm's way while doing my job so I could get back to my littles at home was my main priority.

It was Sinister, Ivy, George and I working together. George recently transferred into the line gang. We had to show him the ropes, and what better way to start than teaching him how to remove and place cables. Our responsibility this evening was reasonably easy. Don't get me wrong; our job was a dangerous one, so you needed to work with a person with the same goal in mind: Getting home to your loved ones. Not sure with whom I'm going to work, I ask the boss. "Sinister is your partner for the evening." We get all of our safety gear and our tools and jump in the first empty pulling truck we see—which meant Sinister and I were going to be the ones removing the cable. The other team, Ivy and George, would be on the watching end, which meant they would be set up in the other manhole watching the cable as we remove it. This was to ensure that nothing was snagged on the way out. If something like that happened, you could cause a cable failure, and our company loved giving you 30 days for little mishaps like that. This job could get you in serious trouble if your eyes and ears weren't open to what was going on, AND…communication is key. I key up my radio and ask where our location is to make sure we are all on the same page. Ivy says, "Southeast 125th Street and Southwest 124th Street."

On the ride to the location, Sinister asks me again, "Are you ok?"

"Yeah I'm good," I reply. "Thank you so much for being my soundboard."

"Sure, no problem," he says, "anytime." And no sooner than he said no problem, he runs it back with, "You can call, and we can talk anytime you like." A door had now been cracked open. Not entirely trusting of Sinister's words, I say ok, but in reality, I knew at that moment I wasn't going to call him. I had already gifted him with too much information. Cynicism had a way with me. Spreading the details of my life was something I never did. I knew it was always best to keep my private life private, but unfortunately, this new world I had a foot in was about to trip me up.

We pull up to the location and immediately jump out to set up the truck. It was a crucial part of the work to safely set up the manhole. The drivers those days were becoming more and more aggressive and impatient. Sometimes we needed to shut down a couple of lanes so we could work safely and adequately. That didn't go over well with some of the people who were in a rush.

Ivy

To say that I admired her would not do my feelings for her any justice. In a crazy way, I looked up to her as some sort of big sister. She had it all—personality, spunk, and lots of charisma. She was an all-around great person. I mean, we all have our flaws, but then again who doesn't?

A thick pretty redbone with bleach blonde hair, and a short cut that, for some reason, she kept putting extensions on. I had asked her why she didn't just let her hair grow. She replied, "Girl, it doesn't matter. I can buy it and put it right back."

She made me laugh. I thought it to be a grievous waste of money, but hey, you like it, I love it. She was also funny. Sinister and Ivy made going to work much more comfortable.

I remember first meeting her in another department of the company. She was the only one who would show me the job. Most of the guys who I worked with didn't want to show me how to complete the work because they wanted me to stay uninformed. Deaf, dumb, and stupid to all aspects of the job so that you were not able to dip into their overtime. As long as you didn't know what you were doing, the managers didn't have to put you on the overtime list because you were deemed unqualified. Of course, none of the managers were coming out to train you; they'd just link you up with a couple of different people, and you'd better sit, watch, learn, ask questions, and hope you pick it up quickly.

"How long have you and Sinister been friends?" she asks me.

"Not long at all, I honestly just met the man. Why?"

"No reason, I was just asking."

I can feel her temperature checking the situation. She was trying to see if something was going on between the two of us. She must have seen

Sinister hug me and then jumped to some conclusion as to our friendship.

"We are just friends" I tell her. Drained from recent events, I tell her that we were talking about something that I was going through. Not wanting to go into details at the moment, I say to her we can talk about it later. No more crying tonight, I tell myself, as I try to concentrate on the job. Although I did sense that there was something in her voice; it was how she asked. Might have even been something in the fact that she had asked, or maybe something was going on between Sinister and Ivy. However, I told myself that it was none of my business.

As we walk back to the truck for a break, she tells me that Sinister reminds her so much of her late boyfriend. Ivy said he talks like him and makes her laugh just like him. Yeah, he's pretty funny I tell her. He's cool people. An all-around good person to be around. Come to find out, Sinister and Ivy's late boyfriend even went to high school together. Except her boyfriend was much older than Sinister. You know what they say, "It's a small world," I told her.

After we took a short break, it was time to get back to work. While getting all the tools ready for the job, Ivy begins to go on and on about the comparison of Sinister and her boyfriend. At one point during our conversation she stops, looks at me, and begins to cry. "Oh how I miss him," she says. I stand there because I don't know what to say. The wound from his passing was still fresh and not too long ago. I don't think you can cover up that much hurt. I didn't know what happened, and I didn't want to be nosey and pry. The best thing I could do for her was to stand there and listen. Just listen to her pain and let her know that I was there for her.

  Slowly we had become friends. As cynical as I was, it was hard for me to let anyone in—especially another female. There is too much backbiting and tattletaling. Too much backstabbing and lying with other females, and that's why I always had a bunch of male friends. I never had to worry about them. They were still going to tell you exactly how they felt regardless. As Ivy talked about her late boyfriend, I just listened. It was heartbreaking to see her in so much pain, and to see her want him back and know that there was nothing she could do. I began to pray for her. It hurt me to see her go through what she was going through. I just prayed that God would release her from her pain. I prayed at that time that she would never have to go through something like that ever again.

Work took us a little over four hours to complete. The next step for us was to get the truck packed up and ready to go, which was an easy task considering that we had a new guy and we had to show him every aspect of the job. Sometimes that slows you down, but he kept up, and we were packed up and on our way back to the garage within an hour.

On the way back to the garage, Sinister asked me how long I knew Ivy and if we were best friends. "No, I wouldn't say we are best friends," I tell him. "However, we are friends. Why do you ask?" "Oh, no reason," he says, "I was just wondering." Instantly I get the same feeling that I got when Ivy asked me about Sinister, and instead of heeding my intuition, I brushed off my gut and kicked it to the curb. Plus, it was none of my business. They could do whatever they wanted to do because I was married. Unhappily married, but married, nonetheless. Wasting any brain power on this was not what I wanted to do. It wasn't relevant to any particular part of my life, but my gut wouldn't let me leave it alone. That door wouldn't close. Something was wrong.

Sinister...Ivy...and Me

Things between Sinister and I quickly escalated. We had become close. He was my best friend, while things between Craig and I plateaued. I was still very much upset with him, and for some reason, I couldn't let it go. The hurt that he caused my child stuck to me and caused me more hurt. How could he not know that something like this would cause me this much pain? It was not some trick to deceive him into submission. I had reached a point where I no longer cared. We never went back to the pastor for any more counseling sessions. He didn't talk about it, and neither did I. It was almost as if he was waiting for me to say I was sorry and we could go back to being us. Except I was now scared that this man could snap at any moment and do this again. He had already shown me what he was capable of, and this time I believed him. No need to speculate, or guess. I saw it with my own eyes, and that was enough for me.

I soon took refuge at work. I took shelter in Sinister. I did everything I could do to avoid the problem I had with my husband. Talking to him was extremely difficult, and since I worked during the night, it was easy. I'd sleep during the day and work at night. We were two ships passing in the night, and that was just fine with me. It was a break from the eerie silence between the two of us, and a break from how I was feeling. I began to notice that I was mad all the time. Being around him made it even worse, and I was still waiting for an answer from God.

I prayed more because this was something I needed. I remember praying before I got married, "God, I don't want to get married to anyone that doesn't want to know you. That doesn't want to get to know you on a deeper level." Sure enough, Craig got up out of his seat and walked down the aisle of the church that same week and joined. He accepted Jesus Christ as his Lord and personal Savior. I thought, "WOW this is it; this is the one!" It was fate; God knew my heart and heard my prayers. He placed it in Craig's heart, and I knew there was no need to wonder anymore if I was for him and he was for me. Had I asked God was this man indeed for me? No, I did not. There was no need. I believed that it was God showing me. Just like I thought it was God showing me to trust Sinister. So I let down my invisible wall of protection that shielded my heart for so many years.

As friends, Sinister and I did everything together, so naturally I was not even just a little bit concerned about the direction I was headed in, because I thought I had it all under control. I was the keeper of my destiny, or so I thought. He was a welcomed distraction to the unfortunate circumstances that crept up on me. Still, I was set on my divorce and never getting married again. I told myself that giving my all to my children was the best thing I could do at this time. Allow myself to heal and help my son heal was all I kept thinking about, but for some reason that song kept playing in my head; *How did you get here, nobody's supposed to be here.* Deborah Cox is stuck in my head, and I hummed the words.

I was married. I'm married, I keep telling myself. Somehow, I have disconnected from my husband. His actions have caused a block in us. I had built a wall and was pretty satisfied with the overall look of it. No matter how long God gave me to think about what was going on because He was still silent with me, so it no longer mattered. Sad to say, I had begun to make excuses for what had happened and what was going to happen. Intrigued, I told myself that it was time to find out if anything was going on between Sinister and Ivy. I could assume there was, but it was easier to ask. So after work, I asked Sinister if it would be possible to talk to him a little bit. "Sure, no problem, let me just get my keys out of my locker," he said. Minutes later he comes out of the locker room, and we start walking and talking toward his car.

"Let's have a seat if you don't mind." He opens the door to the passenger side of his car. Against all better judgment, I take him up on his offer and have a seat in his car. It's a black 2007 Toyota Camry, tan leather interior. "This is nice, did you spend a lot of money for this?" I ask. "I've been thinking about getting me one of these."

"No, it wasn't expensive at all. I bought it online right next to where I live."

"Well if I firmly decide on this car, I'll be giving you a call for the hook-up."

"Sure no problem," he says, "I've got you covered."

I start to get more than a little nervous, but I figure the next best thing to do is just come out with the question. "Listen, I'm not much of a politician, and I'm not for the beating around the bush, but I do have a question to ask you."

"Okay, go ahead. I'm listening." Sinister seemed just as nervous as I was, and even a little apprehensive, not sure which direction I was coming from.

"We have been flirting for quite some time, right?"

"Yeah?" his voice sounds hesitant.

"What's that about? I mean what's your deal. Aren't you and Ivy in the middle of something?"

"What?" he says. "Why would you say something crazy like that?" I didn't expect such a harsh reply. "I would never, could never, see myself with her. Do you see how she talks to people? She's not a nice person." he says.

"I wouldn't exactly say that, but ok," I say.

"What I mean is, she talks nice to your face, but as soon as you turn your back, she says something different. She has many choice words about everyone in the locker room. I couldn't see myself with a person like that."

"Ok, but I thought you were interested in her when you called me and asked for her phone number, remember?"

"No, we just went out for coffee, and I wanted to ask her a couple of questions. Besides, my best friend is interested in getting to know her a little better," he explains. "But why do YOU ask?" he says questioningly as he quickly deflects the conversation off of himself and Ivy.

"Well, it seems like you want something, and I'm not sure where this is heading, so I'd rather ask than assume."

"I do want something, and I think you already know. We have been flirting back and forth for a little while now, but the one thing that has prevented me from taking the next step is, you're married. Soon to be divorced, I know as you keep saying, and I know that your husband hurt you, but I would never hurt you as he did. We have been friends for some time, and I think you're great. I don't want to get into something that could damage our friendship."

It was at that moment Sinister and I kissed. He looked into my eyes and said, "I'd love to get to know you better." The door had opened wider, and I quickly fell in. All my emotions of anger, and feelings of guilt for not being able to be there for my son melted away with just one deadly kiss.

I wanted to call Ivy and tell her what happened, but on another level I also felt incredibly guilty. I mean even though I was married and getting a divorce, the signatures weren't on the paper. I was never supposed to start something new without closing the chapter on the old. Yet here I was.

Not knowing what would happen, or could happen, I chose to keep it all to myself. This was going to be between Sinister and me, but I knew at some point I was going to have to tell Ivy. She was going to find out anyway because I was the type of person to wear my feelings on my sleeve. Hiding what I was thinking or feeling was difficult for me.

I wanted to tell her because we were friends, but somehow I was ashamed of what was going on. The ink wasn't dry on the divorce papers, and the truth of the matter was that I was still married. I hadn't even talked to a lawyer in spite of the recent events that had happened. I kept telling myself to wait on God. Wait on the LORD. Working with each other for as long as we did, we could almost call one another friends and family; more like a family away from family. Unimportant as it may seem, these were the people who had your back. The ones who made sure you were able to go home to your family at night. Unfortunately, for me, I let my guard down.

Keep reading, I'll explain.

I don't believe that Ivy would judge me if I told her what I had hidden, locked away tight. I had already judged myself. I already knew it was wrong. Still, above it all, I felt justified. I trusted Craig with my life. My children were the air that I breathed and were my everything, and he put Gabriel's head through the wall. I can still see it clear as day. An image that is forever imprinted in my thoughts like a baby chick will forever know its mother. I can see it, every single little thing that happened, and these images and sequence of events have now fueled my fire and ordered my steps. He has robbed me of my safe place. He has forced me to lock up my heart and now put my love on trial.

With every intention to speak with Ivy, I ask her to go to lunch.

"I know this great diner that we can go to; would you like to go to lunch or early dinner before work?" I ask Ivy.

"Sure, I'm hungry most of the time before we go to work anyway."

I ask her to meet me at Gemini Diner on 34th Street and 2nd Avenue. There wasn't any place to park, but I loved their salads. They were bright, vibrant, and healthy. My favorite was a cobb salad. Sometimes I'd even ask them to add spinach leaves or romaine lettuce instead of the usual iceberg. The greenery was a necessity for me since the doctors told me that I was a little anemic.

Inside, we sit there talking about everything from the beginning of the shift up until this very moment—just simple conversations about our day. I never tell her all the details about Craig and me because every time I talk about what happened, it makes me cry, and I don't want to bombard her with my tears. I keep it all to myself, and the only people that know about what happened are Craig, Sinister, Gabriel and me. It's just best to keep it that way for now, until I feel strong enough to explain what happened. So we sit and laugh a little while longer before it's time to take the drive to the garage to start another night of work.

All the while, Sinister is continuously on my mind. He takes away the pain.

I'm stuck on the way he makes me laugh. The way he can bring a smile to my face, and he doesn't even know it. I don't tell him how I'm feeling, because I don't want him to make a big deal out of this. Honestly, I'm drunk on the happy: happy moments, happy smiles, happy heart, and happy happy. It felt good to smile and not feel the hurt. Not feeling the guilt of not being able to protect my child. All I kept thinking about was the "what ifs". What if he died? How would I go on? How would the earth continue to turn? Could I keep rotating with the world that I was placed in, or would I give up? My stomach is in knots as I regurgitate that possibility of my world coming to a sudden end, and Gabriel's world coming to an immediate end.

Ivy says she needs to tell me something.

"Could you see yourself being with someone from the job?" she asks.

"No," I tell her quickly, with Sinister on my mind.

"Oh, really? Sinister seems like a terrific guy." I shake my head in agreeance, wondering where in the world she is going with this. "Yeah, but he just reminds me so much of my ex. He died in a car accident you know and he and Sinister act just alike. It's hard sometimes because I think about him. I see Charles in his eyes. I see the best friend that I once had. The best friend that I miss."

"I know what you mean," I tell her, even though I did not. Not a single one of my significant others had ever died. I can hear the pain in her voice, and also understand the longing for more time. However, I had never lost anyone as she had. I didn't have anything else to say. So I agree and hope she changes the subject for fear that she might be able to see how I felt. No one needed to know.

And it was at that moment that I wanted to run. Run for the hills from it all. This situation was all the way wrong, but so was I.

In the next following months, things between Sinister and I began to heat up. It was just nice to hang out with him. His presence was all that kept me sane at that time. The distraction from a life that was no longer happy-go-lucky was all I told myself I needed to keep moving forward. Soon my feelings changed. Possibly because I didn't want to be where I was, perhaps the lust of love, or maybe it was because I did care. I was happy again. Sinister took the place of all the hurt. It was his laugh that made me smile again. And just like that, I knew what I had to do. It was time to put in the paperwork to make it official. Sinister knew how I felt because I finally told him. I didn't want to hide anything. I was tired of keeping everything bottled in, and it was much easier to say how I felt. "I'm getting too old for the games," I told myself. "I have no time to play these kids games anymore."

At some point, you have to live your best life, and I never wanted him ever to come back to me and say I had no idea this is how you felt, or I never knew that this is what you meant. Life at home was very rocky. I never felt at ease anymore, and I would be more than wrong to keep up this lie. What I was doing was wrong. I knew that from the moment Sinister's lips touched mine. I had been convicted many, many times, and I rationalized with God as to why I thought my actions were the best way to handle things. He never gave me a definitive answer as to the future of my life, so I took it upon myself to go down the road less traveled.

I said another prayer and hoped that God would answer me. "God, please show me who this man is. Show me God who Sinister is. I can't get it wrong again." Not confident that God was going to answer my prayers about Sinister because He had not yet answered my prayers about Craig, I still prayed and asked.

As I sit in my car making the final decision concerning how I'm going to handle things, Ivy taps on my window.

"Hey, do you mind if we talk?"

"No not at all," I say. Of course, in my mind, I'm wondering what on earth this could be about. She tells me that she will text me because it was a little late and we had to start work.

"Ok, no problem. Let's get ready for work."

I go into the locker room to change my clothes and try to hurry up so we can talk. We had been talking earlier about Ivy meeting someone. I knew that it was going to take her a long time to love again. Losing someone doesn't make it easy. I just really wanted her to be happy. So naturally, it was nice to hear that she had found someone. I remember on several occasions that she would cry. She would start reminiscing about her good old days. The times she had with him and the things she used to do. I felt terrible for her. I just wanted her to be happy, and so I prayed and asked God to change her situation to fix her broken heart and help her to love again.

We walk out of the locker room ready for the night's work. Time had somehow gotten away from us because it was time to leave the garage and we were not working with each other.

"Hey, I'll text you what I wanted to tell you so that we can leave to get to the work site," Ivy says.

"Sure no worries. I'll wait," I tell her. I had no idea what she wanted to discuss, but I was hoping for the best for her. She had a hard way of it for such a long time.

With all my gear in hand; flashlight, tool belt, safety jacket, helmet, and coveralls, I climb into the work truck. My partner for this evening was Ray. A Filipino man of average height, he had jet black hair and was also a veteran of the Marines. At some point, I remember we talked about him wanting a better life, and he figured going into the Marines would usher him in the right direction. How he wound up in the phone company, I never asked. He always drove the truck about 90% of the time. We had a deal. The partner of whoever drove the truck had to go in the manhole. I didn't mind going in the manhole most of the time, unless I hadn't gotten any sleep the day before. Because we were partners, it wasn't always set in stone, but we often tried to work with each other. Some days if I had a long day of running errands or anything, he wouldn't mind driving and going in the manhole.

My phone goes off. It's a text message from Ivy.

Ivy: *Hey*
Me: *Hey what's up*

Ivy: *I don't even know where to start*

Me: *Try the beginning. It's usually the best part.*

Ivy: *Well, you know I've been seeing someone for a while*

Me: *Yeah, you told me it was a friend of yours, right?*

Ivy: *Yeah, I've known him for a long time*

Me: *Where did you meet him?*

Ivy: *I met him at work...I know I told myself that I would never deal with anyone at this job, but it just happened. He's been after me for a long time.*

Me: *OKAY...who is it?*

Curious, and scared at the same time, I say a little prayer again, "Lord please don't let her say Sinister." I was shaking inside, and it felt like forever for her reply.

Ivy: *It's Sinister. He's been after me for a long time, and I finally decided to give him a chance.*

Instantly, I have an ache in the pit of my stomach, and it feels like I was about to throw up. I feel it coming up slowly. I close my eyes as if this will all go away. What in the world is going on? "Let me get a level head maybe I didn't read the text right," I tell myself, even though I know that I did. Sinister is away for the weekend at his Mother's birthday party. She just turned 70. How convenient for him. We text each other until we reach the work location. I make as much small talk as possible.

"Please don't say anything to anyone," she texts. In my mind, I start thinking that maybe she is trying to get info out of me about Sinister and I. Maybe I wasn't as good as I thought with hiding my feelings. This was all a lie. Sinister always said she had a sneaky way about her, but why now? Sinister always said she was still trying to come up, but not in a hard-working way. Ivy was a hustler. Anything to try and get ahead, but not the right way—not the honest way. I switch to autopilot and drift through the night. Of course, as we worked, all I could do was think about her text. I must have reread it about one hundred times that evening. Each time I did, it never looked any different. *Yes, it's all real*, I tell myself. It's all true, but first I need to talk to Sinister.

So I send him the text: *We need to talk!*

I just wanted to find out if it was true. For some reason, I couldn't believe Ivy. He texts back that he will call in the morning. For the next couple of hours, I patiently wait.

In the morning he calls me just like he said he would. I'm standing in the kitchen when the phone rings. I'm standing in the same spot where Craig threw my boy under the table. Quickly, I make sure to get right to the point. Beating around the bush or making any small talk was pointless. Are you and Ivy sleeping together?

"What? NO!" he says.

His voice sounded annoyed, as if I'm asking some outrageous question. Then he proceeds to ask me why I'd ask him something like that. I tell him, "Ivy said you guys are sleeping with each other."

"She's lying! We already went through this. Why do we have to talk about this? I already told you, I'm not interested in her." Then he proceeds to do what he normally does and bash her some more. It was something in his voice this time that I no longer trusted. He tells me he will call me back, and I say ok because I don't want to talk about it anymore. We hang up the phone and not even two minutes pass and I get a text.

Ivy: *I asked you not to say anything. We said we wouldn't say anything to anyone, but I thought I could trust you*

It was at that moment that I knew she was telling the truth. Right after she texted me, I texted Sinister that I wanted to sit down and talk with him face to face. I had to see him lie to my face. I had to hear him try to play it off one more time. Not to catch him in anything, but to give him one more chance. If Sinister even cared about me as much as he said he did, there's no way in this world he could ever do something like this. The next two days Sinister takes off from work. I wait patiently to talk with him. All sorts of questions pop into my head, and I want the answers, but I don't want the answers because it will be too painful to hear. The truth is, when I first met Sinister, it was something about him that didn't sit right with me. My first impression was that he was a player. As I got to know him, I let my guard down and threw away my discernment. Threw caution to the wind and stepped through the crack in the door. Even still, I decided to get to know him a little more. It was a choice that I made, and one that I was beginning to regret. Hearing God say, "I TOLD YOU SO" was the last thing I wanted to hear. I wanted Sinister to say it wasn't true, and I wanted THAT to be the truth. In my heart, I had all the answers that I needed, but I needed to hear him say it.

Traveling to his apartment seemed like the longest trip I had taken in my life. The commute to Sinister's apartment was a short 45 minutes from my house, and as I got closer, the anxiety of the conversation caused me so much stress it felt like my heart was about to explode. I could feel it banging around in my chest. I could hear it in my mind, and my palms were dripping with sweat.

I knocked on his door. He lived on the bottom floor of an apartment building in a studio. Suddenly, I'm taken to the time when he picked out the apartment. He brought me by to see what I thought.

I stand at his door knowing I must do this, even though I don't want to. "Knock knock knock." He opens the door, and I can see the kitchen. On the counter are two glasses of red wine. I'm jolted to the memory of the pink substance at the bottom of the bottle of the Kendall Jackson.

"Come in," he says, "I poured you and I a glass of wine." Stepping through the door, I look around to see wine bottles all over the place. Two boxes on the floor filled to the top.

"You drink too much. Have you considered slowing down just a bit?" I say.

"Yeah, I know. I am."

He sounds as if I just scolded him. "Come, let's sit down on the couch." We walk over to the couch that I picked out, and suddenly I am not too fond of the brown color. I hate how it feels against my skin. He extends the glass of wine to me. My stomach is turning. I don't want to take even one sip. I'm afraid to take a sip because I might not be able to think. I needed to be able to process these thoughts. No, I don't want anything to drink.

"I need to hear it. Please tell me the truth!" Sitting there begging him to tell me the truth hurt, but I knew that this conversation had to happen and I had absolutely no expectation of what was going to be said. I just wanted to know, and as quickly as I asked, he said, "Yes, we did. Yes, I did."

I look around the room. I can't breathe. The tears are coming, and I can feel them. I don't want him to see me cry, but I can't help it. Then I vomit at the mouth, and every question I can think of comes flying out.

"Does she know about us?"

"YES," he said.

"And what did she say?" I asked.

"She said you'd get over it!" Without even the slightest hesitation in his voice.

"Ok, I have to go," I say to myself. "That's it!"

I didn't want answers. They were questions to make Sinister think about his actions. The memories of all the excuses came to me.

"I thought you couldn't stand her," I say.

"Yeah, I know what I said, but she's changed," he says without looking at me.

"She changed?" my voice gets louder. "How?"

I feel claustrophobic, and I turn my back toward him. Facing the kitchen, I scan the room. I can see myself hurting him. The thoughts play out in my mind like a horror flick. I know I need to leave before I do something stupid. So I get up and walk to the door. I fumble with the door. If I were being chased, my life would have been over. The locks prevent me from leaving.

I'm was so angry I couldn't unlock the door. He asks me to wait, but I know if I stay, orange will be my new black. The door finally opens, and I can't get to my car fast enough. I didn't know where I was going to go. I just wanted to run away. So I drove.

About 20 minutes passes by and I find myself sitting at work in the garage crying my eyes out. Ivy's car comes rolling in right after mine about 10 minutes later. I didn't realize the time. It was almost time for work. I had no intentions of going to work because I knew there would be tears involved and I knew I wasn't going to be able to work effectively with all this on my mind.

Ivy taps on my window, "Can we talk?"

No, I have nothing to say to you, I say in my mind, but instead I say, "Ok."

"I had no idea, I feel like I've just slept with my sister's husband," she says to me.

I sit quietly as Ivy tells me all about her and Sinister and everything they had been doing. There came a time when I didn't even hear her anymore. I knew she was lying, and I no longer wanted to listen to what she had to say. Then she finally said, "He told me that I helped him get over you."

Inside I think to myself, *I thought you just said you didn't know.* It no longer mattered. None of this was right. It all sounded wrong. Somehow the two of them got together and formed a plan as to how they were going to deal with me, I thought.

While I sat there half listening to what she had to say, I watched her demeanor. It didn't bother her one bit that I had been with him. She was not angry, and she didn't sound agitated—not even one single tear. She was calm. We had been working side by side with each other for a couple of years, and it didn't faze her one single bit. I could hear it in her voice that she was not sorry. She could care less. She was saying the words just to say them.

After she finishes telling me everything, she suggests that we both speak to Sinister together; however, I had nothing more to ask or say. She says ok, I get out of the car, and then we go to work. Halfway through the work day, I fake like I'm sick and go home a hot mess. The whole way home all I can think is, I SHOULD HAVE LISTENED TO GOD. I should have listened to Him when he told me it wasn't safe. Sinister was not safe. Craig wasn't safe, and neither was Ivy. I decided to escape one affliction, and unfortunately found myself right in the middle of another. I had jumped out of the frying pan and into the fire. This time it affected my work. I should have listened to GOD when He showed me who Sinister was. I knew I wasn't supposed to be there, or anywhere with him. The pain had a way of changing my mind and switching every rational thought process. We all eat lies when our hearts are hungry, and my heart was starving.

Chapter 4

Lord, Check Please

During the attacks, there was nothing I could do. I felt so out of control and weak. There was no way for me to fight back. There was no way for me to get away. I was a puppet on a string, and my puppet master was some sick, deranged human being that decided this was the best way to get sex and answers. I can almost guarantee that he thought I was never going to remember. Now, I can only speculate as to what was going on in his mind at the time, but I believe he thought that the drugs he had given me would keep me unconscious of his insidious plan.

"How much do you weigh?" Craig asked me one day, as I'm unaware of his intentions at that time. I lied and gave him my weight goal. I told him I was 125, but in reality, I was 10 pounds heavier. I didn't lie to him because I was ashamed of my weight, I lied because it was where I had hoped to be soon.

"Why do you ask?" I reply.

"I just wanted to know. No reason," Craig tells me and then walks away. As quickly as he asked and walked away, the thought left my mind. Thinking back on all his questions and trying to remember the conversations, there was this one thing that he kept saying:

"There are ways to make you tell the truth."

Desperate to have what he needed, a plan had been formed in his mind. Could it have come from someplace else? Of course! I'm sure if you asked him, he would respond that he thought his method was foolproof. I don't know if "he" did this to someone before, or if I was his first victim. However, I do remember that, even if in bits and pieces.

I thought back to the previous conversation when he told me about the time when he went away with his military brothers and one of his friends complained that he woke up and "his ass was hurting."

I wanted to scream at the top of my lungs. Panic, fear, and tears were my new normal.

"For there is nothing hidden that will not be disclosed and nothing concealed that will not be known or brought out into the open." Luke 8:17

My Mother always said, "What's done in the dark will always come to light."

A truth that he assumed I was not telling him. His truth that with his actions he wanted to be kept from me. A truth that keeps me locked up and in chains. Now I ask myself, is he justified? Which road do I take now? Which way do I turn?

"How in the world did this happen to me?" Trapped in the very cortex of my mind, I try once again to retrace my steps.

"Why did this happen to me?" plays over and over. I cry out from the place where only God can hear me. From the pit of my soul where only He knows.

"Why Lord, why me?" I can't but help to ask.

"Why did you let this happen to me?"

I prayed:

"Lord you are my rock. You are my comforter, but I don't feel comforted. My heart is heavy, and I feel like you have abandoned me. You let him do this to me, and when I call out to You, You're nowhere to be found!"

Afflicted constantly, because of the hurt, my mind was cloudy. I couldn't think, there was so much confusion. One minute I'm angry with God, and the next, I feel peace. Angry for what He let happen, and peace because I finally know the truth about what has been happening to me. ANGER is such a strong word, but it's really how I feel. The rage inside of me is at a melting point, and my insides were now crying out for justice. I want to take God to court. He needs to be put on trial. A man that I once loved has violated me. Then he bragged about it on Facebook. Not only that, but my Heavenly Father stood by and watched it all happen and did nothing. GOD is an accomplice to this.

What doesn't kill you makes you stronger, he posts.

Now the record player begins to play my song, round and round it goes. I start to replay all the hurt again and again. Yes, I start to bother myself again with the many details of months that don't supply me with the closure that I desperately need. The closure that I desperately want. I needed to understand. Would jail time be too good for him? Would it be enough? The sentence for the crime that

Craig committed is about ten years, but according to a survey done by The Department of Justice in 1992, he'd likely only have to serve five years. Furious with this type of a slap on the wrist, there is only one place that I can go. I had to go to God on him. Except I was still angry at God for my present-day circumstances. You see, I had started to blame God for what was going on in my life. He had allowed this to happen to me. I told myself over and over that He allowed this. Could this have been because of Sinister and me?

We will get to this question in a moment. Justified, I'm sure he felt he was in the right to do what he did because I cheated on him. I too can claim to be justified because he put my son's head through a wall. Is one sin any greater, or lesser than the other?

"God, I just need to know, Why did you let this happen to me?"

A feeling of abandonment still holds me hostage. I feel like God left me. "He left me unprotected, by this crazy person," I tell myself.

The Bible says, "And the Lord, HE is the One who goes before you. He will be with you; do not fear nor be dismayed." Deuteronomy 31:8

The truth is, God did go before me and protect me. In the memories of these events, I can remember being out of breath constantly. As if someone was choking me, or maybe it was the effect of the medicine. It's not clear, but I do remember I began to cough constantly. My mind tried to rationalize the events and I thought I was getting sick, but I was far from the truth. Even knowing what the Scripture said, I was still a mighty mess. My life had turned upside down again in a matter of a month, and I honestly thought it was over. I wanted it to be over. The one thing that I feared most had happened to me. I was raped, and I had no idea how to handle it. There were so many thoughts racing through my mind. I was angry, sad, furious, depressed, scared, but mostly angry. The kind of anger where you feel a burning in your chest. A tightening in your throat that you can't control. I couldn't hear a single thing. It felt as though my heart was about to leap out of my body and say, "Forget it, I give up!" I was angry at GOD, and my feelings took over. It felt like He left me. Like He took a night off when He was watching me. I felt like He let the enemy sneak into my life and find out what I hid in my heart to protect myself. I had not told anyone that precious secret. No one knew except me and GOD. That was the one thing

I feared the most in this entire world, and the enemy found out.

Oh, how I cried. Crying became second nature to me. I'd brush my teeth and cry. I'd cook dinner and cry. I'd drive to work and cry. I'd cry and cry and cry and cry...nothing made the water stop. I couldn't turn off the hurt, and nothing else mattered to me. My everyday thoughts were consumed with what had happened to me. Never had I felt so alone in all my life. I felt broken. At least that's what I thought. I was that glass vase that had fallen on the floor and shattered into a million pieces. There was no glue. There was no "I'm sorry" either, or anyone there to pick up the pieces. Life to me was over.

I wanted to kill myself.

I began to listen to the thoughts in my head telling me I wasn't needed. The enemy had convinced me that God didn't love me, and the fact of the matter was that GOD DID LOVE ME. I didn't want to live with the guilt and shame of what had happened, and even though it was not my fault, it still happened. The pain that I was feeling, the pain that I felt was so consuming. Every part of my body ached. Not the type of physical pain that can heal like a broken bone or a sprain. It was internal. You couldn't soothe it with "It's going to be Ok" or "Stop thinking about it." Like one of my friends said to me. Her exact words were, "GET OVER IT." I don't know, maybe she thought she was showing me tough love, but her insensitive comments made me sink more and more into seclusion. What if the whole world thinks I needed to get over it? I began to isolate myself. I felt like no one would understand how I was feeling, what was going on in my mind, or how much pain I was actually in. Not even I could explain it. It was horrible, and I never had a clear thought. I just wanted to crawl up into a ball and go to sleep for the rest of my life. I remember talking with my husband, Chris, that it would be just fine with me if I fell asleep and woke up when all the pain was over. Of course, this was improbable, but pain has a way of making you lose your mind.

Chris is 6'2" tall, fit, muscular build. As if he should have been Mr. America, he was a big man. Working out in the gym was his passion. He would go and stay all day if he could, and it didn't matter if it was raining, snowing, or even if there was a hurricane on the way. Nothing was going to stop him from going to the gym. I met him when my best friend at the time asked if I wanted to go to Essence

Fest. At first my thoughts were to decline her offer, because I believed that people only go to these things to meet people and sleep with them. I was not interested in that. However, in this particular year, since things were not going well, I decided to go and take a little vacation with the girls and have fun. Fun was what I needed, I told myself—anything to keep my mind off of everything.

When we first landed, everyone was in such a rush to get to the hotel so we could throw our bags down and see what this festival was all about. One step from the hotel entrance, we quickly found out. There were so many people outside; you could barely walk down Canal Street. There were people everywhere. Sharon, my best friend's cousin, had a friend who she wanted us to meet. Paul was a police officer. She was talking with him on the phone as we navigated toward where he was stationed. My first reaction to the noise and extremely large crowds of this festival was of culture shock. As I quickly acclimated to my surroundings, Chris rolled by in his squad car. He pulled over to talk with Paul, but as soon as he exited his vehicle, I was floored. I couldn't stop staring at him. I was so amazed by his size, and boy was he fine!

Chris kept telling me that I would be ok, and that it was going to take time. However, the pain lingered like a black cloud over my head. It was always an intense feeling. It was always there, hovering.

According to Webster's Dictionary, the meaning of pain is explained as:

-The physical feeling caused by disease, injury, or something that hurts the body.

-Mental or emotional suffering: sadness caused by some emotional or mental problem.

-Someone or something that causes trouble or makes you feel annoyed or angry.

My pain was a combination of all three. The physical pain was over, but the mental pain had just begun.

When you tell someone that you're in pain, they immediately start giving you the once-over to see where you might be in pain. Incidentally, how do you see the pain inside? Not many people can, and not many people try. I only wanted the pain to stop.

My brain was in overdrive, and I couldn't shut it off. I couldn't stop any of the thoughts.

"How could this have happened to me?" I wondered.

"Why hadn't God protected me?"

"Did He really take a night off?"

I began to meditate on all these crazy questions day and night. I didn't get a moment of rest. Even as I slept, my dreams were further tormenting, and my mind was always on what had happened to me. I wanted it all to make sense. I wanted the "why?!" I wanted to know how it all happened. I felt like I needed to know every single sick mean twisted detail of what had taken place. There was no rest for me. It would not come until these questions were answered, and now my days and nights would begin and end with me opening the door of this rape incident and examining every nook and cranny of what I remembered. Like a broken record player, these scenes were on repeat. Round and round in circles I went, hoping that I could remember a little bit more. I meditated on the toxic thoughts that the enemy was consistently feeding me, and there was no rest for me. I was tired, but finding the answer was more important. It never dawned on me how the devil had me. I was no longer in control of my thoughts. Except I thought I was. All day long I heard why?

WHY ME?

WHERE WERE YOU, GOD?

GOD DOESN'T LOVE YOU!

GOD COULDN'T LOVE YOU IF HE LET THIS HAPPEN TO YOU!

WHY DIDN'T YOU PROTECT ME?

GOD DOESN'T LOVE YOU!

GOD DOESN'T LOVE YOU!

Then I began to get angrier. Much angrier than before. I was so tired of the torment that I felt I knew what I had to do. So I drank. I drank and drank and drank until I couldn't think anymore. Until my head was spinning and I could no longer think about the who, what, and where. I had a half jar of liquid encouragement, and it was time. It was time for God and me to have a conversation. My drink of choice for this night was moonshine, and my intentions, I figured I would go out with a bang.

"We are confident, I say, and willing rather to be absent from the body, and to be present with the Lord. 2 Corinthians 5:8

I had been thinking about it for some time now, and I was ready. My heart yearned for the answers to these questions so much so that taking my life so I could be with my Heavenly Father seemed like the best solution to my problem. To me, it was the only way to get my questions answered. I knew Craig wasn't going to tell me. He kept telling people that I was crazy. I knew none of his military buddies would tell me, either. So this to me was the "Only" way. As I fiddle around in the closet for the pills I believed he used on me, I stumble and begin to catch myself. The closet I decide to hold up in just won't stand still. I dig deep into my dresser drawer and my hands don't come up with the pills. I get up off my knees and search again. I'm so drunk I can't find them, and I can't remember what I did with them.

I can't think...did I throw them away?

Where could they be?

Why aren't they here?

Then I scream, "Noooooooooooooo! This isn't fair. I'm ready. I'm ready! This isn't fair!"

Tears roll down my cheeks. It soon becomes a constant flow, and I can't stop crying.

That's when I really start talking to God.

"You let him do this to me, and now you won't let me die."

"You knew this was the only thing I was afraid of."

"You knew this was the one thing that would break me."

"You had all control, and You let this happen."

What kind of God are you?

I wasn't holding any punches. God and I were going to have a conversation one way or another.

I screamed, and yes I was actually in my closet. I kicked, cried, and then I lay down on the floor and cried some more. Then, peace took over, and I fell asleep.

Sleep caressed my cheeks and my clothes, and my shoes sang a lullaby as my tears temporarily washed away my anger.

I wake up about 2 hours later, sober and confused. I tapped into my memories to figure out what just happened. "I'm still supposed to be drunk," I tell myself, but I'm stone cold sober, and my mind starts all over again.

The million dollar question that keeps circling in my mind is, *how could I love someone that could do something like this to me*? Naive? Perhaps, but I always thought there were some things that we all would never do. I always thought there were some things my husband could never do. What I know now and see now… we are all capable of it. After what had happened to me. Rage and anger were all I saw, and I was willing to kill because of it. I believe there were more people involved. Not saying Craig is dumb, but his new group of military friends most likely gave him the idea, because this should have happened a million times over throughout the life of our relationship. Who could have helped him? I have no clue, maybe it was the people laughing on the post when he secretly needed to get a nut, or perhaps it's someone I don't even know. At any rate, they will eventually have to pay for this crime, whether it be in this life or the next, and each person will be held accountable. The Bible is marked clear, and its words stare back in black and white:

"So then each of us shall give account of himself to God." Romans 14:12

Chapter 5

How Must I Cope

Job Experience

Making sense of why God didn't help me or fight the good fight for me was crucial to my very existence. At the moment, I was being tossed to and fro by my cynicism. It fueled my vacillating faith and twisted my love for Him. Everything that I knew about God was a lie, and now I wanted answers. I was told in church to always "go boldly to the throne" Hebrews 4:16, and that's exactly what I was going to do. My heart was extremely troubled by my reality, and my mind was being invaded by lies constantly. Each thought crushed my knowledge of who God was to me. Every thought made me take a couple more steps in the wrong direction, and my lack of knowledge helped fuel this cat and mouse game that the devil had begun to play with me.

I was hurting. There was so much pain. My focus was solely on my pain. I had no idea what to do anymore. At first, I thought it was all eventually going to go away, and if I waited it out for a while, I would feel better afterwards. However, I was cast down, and I didn't know it at the time.

The meaning of cast down:

1. To turn downward
2. to be saddened; depressed; discouraged

Swaddled like a newborn babe, I was wrapped in depression. Each moment I felt like I was being held captive by time. I couldn't move forward. I didn't want to move forward, nor did I even care anymore. I never considered myself a quitter; frankly, life just didn't matter to me anymore. The thoughts of suicide were percolating. Even though I had children, the thoughts boiled inside of me. Even though I had a great job, the thoughts simmered. Even though I had more people who loved me than people who didn't, the idea of taking my life brewed. I had finally begun to understand why people took their lives. I was standing on that same ledge.

There are many reasons why people want to commit suicide. Some research shows that when people want to commit suicide, it can be because they can't cope with an issue that has been plaguing them. I don't say this to create some image of a hysterically psychotic, crazed off-the-wall person who can't take life anymore. Yes, we all feel a little down sometimes, but know this: what pains me simply might not hurt you. We are all built differently. I say this to help you understand that we go through different experiences, and some of the issues we experience strengthen us. Some experiences change us, and some of those same issues rock our foundation and make us wish we were never born. This trauma of mine was a faith changer. I likened myself to Job for a short period. For a minimal amount of time, I compared myself to this man who God HIMSELF called blameless. This affliction took my breath away. For me this pain was so intense, it made me want to skip the middle of my life and cut right to the end. It felt as if I'd be stuck in this spot forever.

In the Bible, Job lost everything. The first few chapters give an account of Job's life and his encounter with the devil. Imagine losing everything you had—wealth, your home, and your children—in ONE day. Not only did he lose everything in one day, but the Bible tells us that Job was blameless. I can admit that I AM NOT AND PROBABLY NEVER WILL BE BLAMELESS, but for a little while I compared my experience to that of Job.

I, like Job, lost something on the day when Craig raped me. I became numb to the world. I lost that loving feeling, no pun intended. Nothing felt the same. I was given a new perspective, and at the time, I didn't understand it. Grasping the concept that this had happened to me was hard enough. So I knew that no one was going to fully understand what I was going through, or what was going on in my mind until perhaps they went through it themselves. They can't, and I tell myself even if they say they can. How, if they have never taken a step in either direction of my life? How, if they've never walked a mile in my shoes? In spite of my new apocalypse, I do believe there are a couple of people in the world who are empathetic.

The definition of empathy according to Webster's Dictionary

Empathy:

1. The feeling that you understand and share another person's experiences and emotions: the ability to share someone else's feelings.

2. The action of understanding, being aware of, being sensitive to, and vicariously experiencing the feelings, thoughts, and experience of another of either the past or present without having the feelings, thoughts, and experience fully communicated in an objectively explicit manner; also: the capacity for this.

Now there are people in this world who have the ability to put themselves in your shoes, but they are not many. Our society is all about me, me, me and what I can get from whom, and unfortunately, it fuels a cycle that keeps us going around in circles. We are not able to care for and help each other. We are not able to see when a person is hurting because we are so focused on ourselves.

For most, the thought of suicide is quite scary. To think the person you love; whether mother, father, sister, brother, or best friend - the list can be endless - wants to commit suicide, is rattling. All too often, we ask ourselves, "Why would anyone want to take their own life?" Life is great. Possibly because we cannot see life from their point of view, nor have we experienced life from another's point of view.

I used to say that. "Why would anyone even think about taking their own life? It can't be *that* bad. However, now standing on this ledge of circumstances and hills and valleys of a million regrettable actions looking over, I can relate. No judgment, or even an ounce of criticism - I finally understand. For me, there were two simple reasons why I couldn't cope. The first reason was just that I was in pain. Intense pain that I couldn't shake off. Pain that took all my strength from me.

Pain

My pain was so consuming, I felt like I COULDN'T escape my issues, and at one point it seemed like I was drowning. My pain, like water, constantly surrounded me. I was submerged in the thick of it, and it was as if I was suffocating. The pain I felt, and the tears I cried were endless. Swimming in a pool of tears, each day, I wanted so much to lie down and wake up when my life was over. My will to live had vanished. The good feeling I had of waking up in the morning evaded me. I'd wake up each morning with utter disdain for the sun rising, as the days were not days anymore. Each one blended into the next, becoming one long continuous morning or night. A night that drifted into the morning with no end in sight. No end to the hurt in my heart, no end to the constant heartache, and nothing to help me get over and rid myself of this anguish. My hurt was so intense that I was consumed with trying to find my way out, and at that particular time, nothing else mattered anymore. I wanted so much to understand the reason "why". Why had it happened and why was I not protected? Why me Lord...why ME Lord...WHY ME LORD...WHY?

I remember when I asked those very words "why me?" out loud. Until then I had only thought it in my mind. It was a question that played over and over in my head. I was talking with Chris on the phone while driving to work. I began screaming, "Why…Why...Why...?" this was the only thing. Being raped was the only thing I was ever afraid of. As quickly as I asked the question, he came back with the response; something I was not prepared for. His words cut me deep.

"Why not you?"

"What did you say?" I asked. His words slapped me into a state of acute awareness. *I don't believe I heard him right,* I said to myself.

As I was driving, my eyes opened wide, and I wanted to bring the car to a sudden stop. I was on a patch of highway that would have killed me and anyone in front or behind me if I had followed through with my initial reaction. The tears stopped and I was immediately distressed by what I had just heard him say. Why not you? It was registering, but it was taking an awfully long time. I start hearing my voice say, "Did he say what I think he said?" It began to register gradually. Why not you? I looked at the phone because I couldn't believe my ears. So naturally I needed to ask him, "What did you just say?"

He said, "I said, *Why not you?*"

That was it, a five-alarm fire goes off in my head, and I start screaming and crying even more. How could he be so insensitive? *Does he have any idea what I'm going through?* I ask myself, ready to give him a piece of my mind, but he stops me before the venom begins to flow.

"Are you so special that something like this can't happen to you? Is it your job, or the clothes you wear? What is it that makes you so special that something like this shouldn't have happened to you? What? Is it supposed to happen to someone else and not you? Why them and not you?"

I can feel the anger filling my lungs as I take a breath, and if I could at that moment, I would have probably stopped breathing. I begin to scream. It's not fair. This does not seem right. Suddenly, it comes to me, and I say to Chris, "He's going to get away with this. Every single thing that he has done. He's going to get away with all of it."

There's no one to catch him and not enough evidence to convict him and throw him in jail. So now he gets away scot-free. Now what? I begin to start crying more. Now, what do I do? The floodgates have opened, and I can't even see out the windshield. I try to wipe away the tears, but another one quickly takes its place. In a quiet, soft voice, he tells me to calm down, and then he says, "He's not going to get away with anything. He has to pay for his crime, in this life or the next. We must all give an account for our lives, and on the day of judgment, he will have to do the same." His words don't help soothe the sting of the bandage that he just ripped off my heart. "How do you know? Maybe I deserve this. Every bit of pain and torment that is going on right now." "Shhhhhhhhhh," he says to me, let us pray. In a mid-rage, he quiets my soul with that one word...pray. Pray? What were we praying for? Prayer was the last thing on my mind. God and I were not friends. We weren't even on speaking terms.

He speaks...

"Lord, we just want to say Thank you. Thank you for all that you are doing at this very moment for us. We come before you at this exact moment with specific prayers to help Denise, Lord. Right now she is hurting, Lord. Right now we come to you for healing. Please heal all the hurt in her heart, if it is in your will. Right now, please calm her mind and give her peace. We don't understand why some things happen, but we know You are still in control. Please, in your time Lord, and in your way, enlighten her as to the specifics of this pain. Help her to understand the why of it all. Lord, if it is not in Your will that she understands, please we ask that you give her the strength to keep going. To keep putting one foot in front of the other. Give her the strength to trust in You, Lord. In your Son Jesus' name, we pray, Amen."

"Amen," I say.

Suddenly, just like that, I was no longer enraged. Instantly, the load wasn't as heavy. Don't get me wrong, I was still angry with God, but it was the fact that he prayed for me. No one had ever prayed for me before. Anger had somehow clothed my heart, but it was as if a chunk of rage had been removed. The sting of it was gone.

We talked for a little while longer until I reached the garage entrance of my work location. We had changed the subject and started talking about something else. I was half-listening because I was unable to let Chris' question go. "Why not you?"

Most of my life I considered myself to be a happy-go-lucky person. Nothing bothered me. I was able to shake off whatever it was that disturbed me, but not this time. It was this one single offense that vexed my soul. Not for a day, not for a year, as I still live and breathe at this moment that it doesn't torment me. It has taken me such a long time to get to this point, but seriously now I had to sit back and ask myself why I was so angry. Why was I so angry with God? What was it that I had been angry with Him about? Who is truly to blame? Like Chris said, "Why not me?" I had to think about this for a moment. The hard questions needed to be asked and answered. First thing I needed to do was reflect upon myself. As I begin to think about this question, I tell myself not to cry, but I can't help it. These tears I cry, and have cried, God says He stores in a bottle:

Thou tellest my wanderings: put thou my tears into thy bottle are they not in thy book. Psalms 56:8

As I began to think about the questions again, I felt like I had to make him understand why I was feeling the way I felt because I couldn't understand why he felt the need to ask me that question. No, I wasn't so special that this couldn't happen to me, but it was the one thing that I hid in my heart so no one would be able to hurt me. Sticks and stones is a crucial lesson that we teach our children, and I learned that early. You could say anything you wanted, and it didn't matter, as long as you didn't put your hands on me. We try to teach our children to let their peers say whatever they want until they make that one crucial bad decision to put their hands on you and then there is no telling the teacher - it's time to defend yourself. There was no teacher for me. Whom was I supposed to meet for the rectification of this situation? There was only one who I could go to, and I was fighting mad that this was something He allowed. Did God want me to be in pain? Why had God allowed this to happen to me?

Keep reading—we will get to that shortly.

The second reason a large number of people want to commit suicide is because of an inability to cope with the issues and circumstances of what has or is happening to them. A disability so crippling that you are not even aware of the problem until you are paralyzed. An event that has rendered you frightened and helpless. That was me.

Did you know that suicide is the 10th leading cause of death in the United States? Each day approximately 123 people die by suicide, and according to the The Center for Disease Control and Prevention, every 12 minutes someone tries to take their own life and succeeds - not just all over the world, but here in the United States. Nearly 8,000,000 people die each year by suicide—that's one death every 40 seconds in the world as a whole! Suicide happens to be the 2nd leading cause of death in the world. The number one cause of death in the world is heart disease. There are so many people suffering in silence, so many who are not able to cope, some who have absolutely no idea where to turn; and when they do, there's a stigma attached because now you're crazy. Whether depressed, sad, uneasy, in pain, or hurting. They always attach *crazy* to the end of it to make themselves feel better. These are the people who are not able to cope, and these same people sometimes believe that the world would be just fine without them. I thought this same way for a long time.

And for a long time I was afraid to tell anyone how I felt. It was best to keep this sort of thing to myself, because at the very moment that you tell someone, with the hope of ending your suffering and pain, they start to think you're crazy. I thought I had to keep it to myself. I didn't want anyone to know what had happened to me. The embarrassment of the whole situation and what he had been doing and done to me grieved every inch of me. I began to tell myself it was all my fault. It's my fault that it happened. It's my fault that I can't remember all the details. It's even my fault that he got away with all that he has done.

Wrapping my mind around the fact that this had happened to me kept me walking on that long road of isolation. Pondering, day in and day out, why I couldn't see this coming, and try to make provisions to catch him in the act. It continued that I blamed myself for the disgusting things that he had done to me. I had pushed him to the edge, forced his hand, and MADE him rape me. I can almost guarantee that this is the way he felt, but it's only my opinion. Stepping out on my husband and seeking some comfort in "Sinister" at work had caused him to lose his mind, right? Maybe the devil made him do it? Perhaps it was just pure revenge. Maybe, just maybe, this was the person who I married, and sooner or later it would have happened. Regardless of his mental state and participation in how he decided to seek the truth, as he so called it, I regret my actions. I regret that Sinister's mother ever had him. Although it's not his fault what happened to me, I wish like crazy I could say the devil made ME do it, but the truth of the matter is the devil can't make you do anything. He can make suggestions, a whole lot of suggestions, but he can't make you do a single thing. Remised, I must admit he is crafty.

  I remember each day I'd come home tired from work, and I'd have to cook because he didn't know how, and then I'd have to clean the house as well. Telling him over and over that we were in this together did absolutely nothing. None of that mattered….nothing. He did not hear a single word. Nothing I did encouraged him nor made him better in any way. I was exhausted, tired from giving and my efforts not achieving their goal. I was tired of giving and not seeing any change. This might be the part in this book where you side with Craig and assume that I had gotten what I deserved—hoorah, you chant and laugh because of the brotherhood.

Please read on.

It might not have been the correct way to handle things. However, I can tell you that my life didn't come with a manual, or so I thought. It was a little hard for me, doing as much as I was doing. I began to feel unappreciated, and at that time all I wanted out of this was better sex and a little help around the house. He was depressed, and I didn't know what to do anymore, so I just let him be. I hoped he would somehow get his confidence back and come around. We had an earlier conversation where he told me he didn't feel like a man if he wasn't making the most money in the household. No matter what I said, it didn't matter. Telling him things would be ok after he lost his job didn't register. He began to slip away, and with each day that passed, it became harder and harder to reel him back in. He was always angry. The children always made him angry. We had many conversations as to what it was that caused him so much anguish. He claimed he was always fine. I knew that he was taking the loss of his job hard, but I never knew how hard. Was it only the loss of his career that caused him to sit in his pit? From the moment he lost his job, I knew that he was laid low, but I never knew to what extent. And then one day he just seemed to crack. He lost his mind in one split second. Had I known that he was at that level of anger, I would have tried to get him some help.

    Recommending him to go back to the military was just a way to make him feel relevant again. He needed to feel *needed,* and the fact that I had a job - a good paying job - drove him crazy instead of comforting him. It no longer put his mind at ease because I was now the breadwinner. Now the children vexed him and he wasn't appreciating the opportunity that God gave him to form a stronger bond with the littles. Forever etched in every crack and crevice of my mind, I will remember my husband throwing my son all across the kitchen. Like a rag doll, my son flying under the table, and him hitting the cabinets. His little body slammed up against the fridge. Those visions are extremely hard to let go of. It's not something I could wish away. It would be nice to open up my mind and remove that one day. A simple extraction perhaps by the most celebrated brain surgeon in the world, yet sadly that does not exist. Had I not been there to witness this myself, I would have been inclined to call my child a liar if he told me this happened to him. "The Craig I know would never have done this," I said to myself. My memories take me back to that day once more. Craig picks Gabriel up by his neck and slams his head into the corner of the wall and creates a huge dent. He put my son's head through the wall. I scream at him to stop, but he won't take his hands from around his neck, and Gabriel begins to cry.

After watching all of these details unfold, the very first questions that came to mind were, "Who in the world did I marry? What type of person did I marry? What just happened here?" Sitting there in shock, all I wanted to do was pack up my children and run.

Was this what I signed up for when I got married? Was this the "for better, or for worse" part? Was this, "in sickness and in health?" I no longer wanted to think about the answers or wait for them. I left him. I didn't move out. I just left him in my heart and my mind.

Chapter 6

Lord Who Are You

God the Magician

When I was younger, in my early twenties, I began to question who God was. A curious kind of thought, I was left wondering if there was even a God. I'd ask myself, "Who was God?" "What type of God was I being shown to worship?" "Why was I praying?" I was told to worship like so many of us in this world, and not because I wanted to worship God. My Grandmother, the matriarch of our family, made sure we were in church every single Sunday morning. If we weren't there, best believe by Sunday evening, you were getting a call asking where you were. If you weren't sick, then there was nothing you could have said that would have been an acceptable answer. One day, alone, just God and I, I said a little prayer.

"God if you exist, please show me." Short and simple, but to the point. I just wanted an answer.

Thoughts of my past grab hold of me and shake me to a moment when Gabriel was about two years old. My mother and I had decided to go food shopping at our Local Shoprite. Mom was trying to hammer into me the need to make sure that dinner was made by 2 p.m. every day. Why? Possibly because that's the way she was taught and you can't have dinner made without the food, of course. Justin had also decided to go with us. He was four at the time. It wasn't to do a whole lot of food shopping; we just needed to get a couple of things for dinner for that evening.

We quickly pack the boys in my little red Pontiac Lemans so we can beat the evening rush and make dinner in a timely fashion. Before we get into the store, I take the time to have the talk with the boys, "Don't touch anything in this store, and no, you can't have anything." They look at me as if I have two heads and say, "Okay Mommy." My Mom starts laughing, "I wonder where you get that from?" I start with, "Gee I have no idea," while laughing all the way to the front door of the supermarket. Mom and I rush through the aisles because I know how she is. She loves to pick up things that she might need instead of things that we do need. It has always impressed me how she can walk down the aisle and pick up two of this and three of that because you never know we might need it later. Not wanting to spend any more time in the store than we had to, I quickly remind her what we need. She gives me the, "I know, I know, who's the mother here? Me, or you?" reply, and we get it done. The checkout person is very pleasant. She is all smiles when the boys and I start putting all the groceries on the belt. "Oh, how cute." She's looking at Gabriel with his blonde hair. "How old is he?" she asks. "I just can't take my eyes off of him!" Gabriel always had that effect on the ladies.

"Thank you, he's two years old," I respond.

"How did he get that hair? Is his father white?"

I start laughing. "Yes, he is." I stand there ready for the next set of questions that should be coming my way. I didn't mind, but sometimes when I'm in a hurry, entertaining these type of questions was a bit annoying. Just because I was African American, they assume his hair and eyes could not come from anywhere on my side of the family. She proceeds to continue scanning my groceries, and maybe she heard the hesitation in my voice, but we continue, and she says, "Take care of those beautiful babies."

I say thank you again, quickly grab the groceries, and exit the store and make my way back to the car. It was a beautiful day outside. It was absolutely perfect. Not too many clouds in the sky and the temperature was around 70, or maybe 75 degrees; I just remember it wasn't too hot.

On the way home, I tell Mom that I'll put all the groceries away if she brings the boys upstairs. She agrees. I figured a nice compromise was in order because I knew it would be me who was going to make dinner. As I pull up to the house, I let my mom, Gabriel, and Justin out of the car. My mother's house sat on a hill, and her driveway was on an incline. For no reason, but for some reason, this was the day that I decided to park the car in the driveway instead of in front of the house like I usually did day in and day out. Mom gets out of the car, and she and the boys go up the stairs toward the front door. I start my incline to park "little red" in the driveway. Driving up the hill was no problem, but after I pulled the emergency brake on my standard, the car wouldn't hold in the driveway. It kept sliding back, so I tell myself to try again. I drive up a little further in the driveway, pull the emergency brake and yet again the car slides back toward the street. Frustrated, I tell myself to try it one more time, and if it doesn't work this time, I'll just put it in front of the house like I normally did. Again, I drive the car up the hill and try to pull the emergency brake to hold the car. As clear as day a voice says, "Put it in 1st gear and pull the emergency brake, and the car will hold". So, that is exactly what I did. Happy that the car held, I get out and begin to walk down the driveway to go upstairs to start cooking. As I get to the back of the car, I see Gabriel standing there. Directly in the middle of the back of the car. He looks at me with the biggest smile on his face and says, "Hi Mommy." My heart leaped out of my chest and hit the floor. I heard the same voice in the softest sweetest tone, the same voice that told me to pull the brake and put the car in 1st gear say, "See, I'm here." Tears instantly ran down my cheeks. I picked Gabriel up and hugged him like I never hugged him before in my life. There was no question. I would have run over my child. I would have killed him. Had I not listened to the voice, and listened to my feelings of frustration, I knew I would have most definitely run him over.

    I ran up the stairs and started screaming at my mother. "I thought you had him. I thought you were watching him!" I couldn't stop crying. She had no idea what had just transpired. I was so scared and happy all at the same time. It was impossible to process all the emotions that I was feeling. Crying was the sweet release, as my tears became a natural painkiller. Speaking the words of what happened was difficult. I wanted to let her know what happened, but all I wanted to do at the time was hold him and not let him go. I heard the voice of God. He saved my child with just a whisper. I had been told all my life who God was and what God does, but had never seen it firsthand. I have read the Bible and all the stories about who God is, and what He has done for us, but not seen it with my own eyes. That day, I witnessed it. That day I heard Him. That day I heard God's voice. Finally, as the tears slowed, I was able to tell my mother what happened. We stood there for a moment sharing the same reaction. Amazed, I said, "He talked to me." There was urgency in what He had instructed me to do. He didn't yell, but I knew in my heart it was important. Never did I even think to question why He spoke to me; I was just in awe that He did. ME! I had no idea that it was His voice until I walked down the driveway and saw my 2-year-old standing where he was with the biggest smile on his face. I knew the severity of what could have happened. I knew that if I hadn't listened, my son would not be here at this very moment. Yes, I listened. Why? Because it allowed me the opportunity to have my car in the driveway as I wanted. Little did I know, the emergency brake failed because it had broken earlier and I had no idea. It was never going to work. The car was going to keep sliding back.

A New Perspective

God saw this. He held my hand and walked me through what could have been a devastating situation. Had I not listened to what God had instructed me to do at that moment, I know without a doubt, without my faith wavering, and without the smallest bit of hesitation that Gabriel would not be alive today. He would be a memory. I knew deep down within me at that moment I had to find out who God was for myself. I had to know. No more listening to what other people said about God. I decided to find out for myself. I decided to open the Bible and read it. Not for Gabriel or my children, but for me. I had to find out Who had saved my son. That was the beginning of my walk with God.

I opened the King James Bible and tried to read it, but the language was a little hard for me to understand. So I decided to get an NIV Bible. It reads more like a story than an act out of a Shakespeare play. It also facilitated a much-needed understanding that began to help me build the bond between God and me. Of course, it would have been too easy to let it slide and accept that my son had been saved by happenstance, but I knew deep down that I would have been entirely wrong. I heard His voice clearly. There was no luck in what had happened to me. I may not be able to understand at this moment why it happened to me, but it did happen.

Going to church all those years before this incident, I had never really known who God was. I would sit in the pew and try my best to listen to the preacher. He would tell us who God was. "He is a sustainer. He is the great I Am. The doctor in a sick room. The lawyer in a courtroom. God is your all and all." I heard all the stories from beginning to end. He is the sunrise and the sunset. He is the Lily of the valley and the Prince of peace. The Lord of Lords and King of Kings. Abraham, Lot, Moses, Joshua, Jesus. The woman with the issue of blood. However, the "who" of it had all of my attention this time. I was spared an immeasurable amount of pain, and I hadn't the slightest idea why. Elated of course, but I had to ask myself could it have been because God needed Gabriel? Could it have been because He needed his life to go a little further down the road? Could it have been that someone needed

Gabriel more than me? Whatever it might have been, I needed to understand a little more. It was no longer acceptable to have anyone else explain to me who God was. In those seconds that I heard instructions for me, which kept my son safe, I knew I was given a small glimpse of Who God was. Now it was time for me to go a little bit deeper.

Honestly, I could have sat there that day and let it all go. I could have gotten caught up with so many other people who don't want to crack the book open because Massa used the book to keep us African Americans enslaved by beating us down mentally with something that he knew was wrong. I could have allowed the world to shape my view of who God was, but on that day I had to find out for myself. So I started with the Bible. I started with the manual, as Dr. Myles Munroe calls it. I had the pleasure of meeting him during one of his speaking engagements in Tennessee. It was very interesting how he broke it down. God our creator did not leave us without any instructions. The Bible is our roadmap to life. Anything that has been done or has happened in life, has been done or has happened in the Bible. It also shows how to respond to the difficulties of life. He proceeds to explain how pretty much everything that we use has a manual. Television, DVD player, a car, you name it. There are instructions to almost each and everything that we use. Guidance as to how to handle each and everything that we acquire. So why would GOD not leave us with instructions to life? I realize that some people are stuck on the tragedy of 400 hundred years with no acre and a mule. I get it, but you have to read it for yourself. Hence, my initial reaction when I realized what God did for me. It took time, but it was time I wanted to spend learning the details. The world was no longer going to shape my view of who God was any longer.

    My journey started by just reading to understand. I quickly came to a conclusion of who God was and the sacrifice that He made for us all. Imagine giving up your life for a world that doesn't even believe in you, your mission or something so basic as love. Not even I was aware of the magnitude of this great sacrifice. It took me spending time with God to just scratch the surface. Soon, I had a false sense of who God was. If I didn't do anything wrong, or did my best not to do anything wrong, God would protect me. As long as I go to church and praise and worship Him, I will stay under His care! I had it wrong. I was living my life the best way I knew how when the floor opened from underneath me. Yes, God knew my heart, but there was something wrong. Craig and I were not doing well. I knew I would have been wrong, but I also thought that God would understand because of what Craig did to Gabriel. I began to rationalize and pick and choose the good and bad out the Bible to fit my own agenda so that I could do what I wanted to do because things got hard. I no longer wanted to love this man. His actions made him unsafe to love. His actions made me forget everything that I read and learned. The world view was much better, so I slipped back to where it no longer hurt.

    I slipped back to the part where I had heard my best friend telling me, "Go ahead and live your life." The excuse to go ahead and do whatever you want because that is what the world is doing. I wanted God to give me the ok to divorce him. I asked for a sign to let me know that it was ok. That's why I initially waited for His reply, but I determined that God was taking too long. I knew what was best for me, and all I wanted to do was be happy.

    So you can imagine my initial reaction to my circumstances when I was raped. From the very beginning, God was my protector. He saved my son and has woken him up every single day since then. I had given my life to God and accepted Him as my Lord and Savior a short time after he saved Gabriel, and now He had not protected me when I felt that I needed Him the most. These actions had me thinking this was a new God, or so I thought. Maybe this God that I had grown to know was not really who I thought He was. Could I have prematurely accepted God as my Savior, and He possibly was not a savior at all? Tragically, I had it all wrong. I was so confused; one minute I was learning who God was, and the next I thought I had it all figured out.

Yes, I know that God is not a magician. He is not a genie, either. While I studied, I learned that sometimes when we make a request, whether in prayer or just by directly talking to God, we believe that "poof", in a matter of seconds, it will get done. We believe it should get done. We even go as far as telling God how we want it to get done. The trouble with that type of mentality is when it doesn't get done right away, or at all for that matter, we get angry, we lose hope, and we lose faith. I must say, I thought that way for a moment. I wanted so badly for Craig to go to jail that I prayed and prayed that God wouldn't allow him to get away with this madness. I cried even more when I saw him walking around not getting punished for what I believed to be a heinous crime. Craig drugged and raped me. He deserved to go to jail, and I wanted and needed him to go to jail right away. A simple fix, I assumed. So I began to pray that justice would be served. I prayed that my Heavenly Father would see what was done in the dark and bring it to light, and then I waited. To add a little urgency to the issue, I began to fast. All sorts of thoughts came to my mind to do anything to get the job done, and what better way to get the job done than to fast, to "MAKE" God do what I wanted HIM to do. It was either kill him for what he did to me, or plead my case. I gave up something that I loved...coffee. Might not mean much to you, but I loved me some coffee. It didn't necessarily have to be Starbucks, either. McDonald's was just fine with me. For me, it's like a hug in a cup. Naturally, I assumed it would happen right away. I mean, we are talking about God. He can do anything. Also, seeing the nature of this tragedy that had recently taken place, HE would right the wrong. He'd want to right the wrong because God hates sin, and Craig definitely sinned in my eyes. During my coffee fast, a year went by and nothing happened. I would pray and pray and pray. I'd read the Bible to try my best to stay encouraged. It was time for me to encourage myself. Each day I told myself to stay strong. You see, I knew it was going to happen any day, and it was just a matter of time. I told myself it was going to happen as long as I continued to live without something that I really wanted. At the moment, God was busy with a plethora of other people's problems, and it was just going to take Him some time to get to mine. Soon my days turned into weeks, and weeks into months.

Then two years went by, and he was still walking around free as a bird. The thoughts began to surface again, except now I found myself thinking of ways to kill him for everything that had happened. I constantly flip-flopped between still being angry with God and being angry with Craig. A small conversation with my father rectified my thoughts. His exact words, "You wouldn't just be taking one life, you'd be taking five. Why give up your freedom for revenge? Why allow him to make you kill your children too, because that's what you'd be doing. Your actions would possibly alter their lives in a bad way as well." I knew in my heart that he was right. I knew then that I had to wait…wait, I say, on the Lord, and it wasn't easy. It meant that I had to have faith. I had to continue building my relationship with Him, and wait on God to right my wrong. Three years go by, and I'm angry, sad, and hurting all over again. Lord, I want to know why You are taking so long! I'm the one who needs you. Why continue to let him get away with this? And again I hear the voice of God say, "When you were out there doing what you wanted to do, did I stop you? Why is there such a rush now?" I knew God was right, but it was draining. I started asking myself how to shake this feeling that I had. I was still angry with God, and I was not able to address it. I wanted to pray to God to help me, but in reality, I was still angry with Him and the why. My foot was halfway in the door and halfway with Him. I believed in God, but not on Him. I believed God was who He said He was, but I didn't think God would do what He said He would do, and especially not for me. So how was He supposed to answer my prayers? I was that lukewarm Christianity I had heard about; that at first sight of trouble my foundation crumbled. Why would He answer my prayers? Finally, I realized that I needed help getting back to God. Sorely, I came to myself that I thought I knew, but the reality of it was I had no clue who this Lord and Savior was, let alone where He was when all of this was happening.

Like so many other people, I began to question God and His whereabouts when things of this nature suddenly took place. I was left questioning God as to how He was able to let things like this happen. Then I was left asking God if He was even a good God anymore. Children are dying of hunger. There are all sorts of evil things going on in the world, and You are just letting all of this continue without doing anything about it. What good God would allow such suffering?

Chapter 7

God Where Are You

I was depressed, and I was constantly asking God where He was. Where was He when all of this was going on? Had He left me alone and allowed Craig to do as he pleased because I too had sinned? Had He left me because the rape was my punishment? Had God allowed this because it was my turn to be in pain? Did he not stop him from committing this crime because I was the one who was wrong? Because it was my time to suffer? Why hadn't He stepped in to stop this? Question after question, I kept asking and listening for answers, trying desperately to figure out what had happened because none of this made any sense to me and I really wanted it to.

As I sat on the edge of my bed, I KNEW THAT THIS WAS WHERE IT HAPPENED. I had looked at the spot on my bed and remembered his hand ushering me to where he wanted me to be and not allowing me to get away. I take a deep breath and let it out slowly. All I want to do is move far far away, but there is no place I can go. There is no place I can go to stop this hurt. I search my thoughts once again, and my feelings of abandonment add more fuel to an already raging fire. As if God left me during the most crucial part of my existence. It felt like He turned His back on me.

Jesus Himself cried out from the cross.

"And about the ninth hour, Jesus cried with a loud voice, saying Eli, Eli, lama sabachthani? That is to say, My God, my God why hast thou forsaken me?"

During the early years of my journey, I learned that God is omnipresent (EVERYWHERE ALL THE TIME), and God is omnipotent (ALL POWERFUL). He has the ability to be everywhere with everyone at the same time. So if this is true, then I had to ask again where God was. I had to pray and ask God where HE was when Craig was doing what he was doing. My feelings had me. "Joyce Meyers quotes"

Does God Love Me Anymore

Chris and I had talked about this many, many times. I had explained on a number of occasions to him that God left me. Chris knew how I felt, and I'm forever thankful that he had a level head during this time. I felt unloved. In my mind, God wouldn't have abandoned me if the rape didn't come to fruition. God had forsaken me. If God had stopped this from happening and somehow saved me from it all, then God did love me, and He would have been my protector once again. However, God did allow this to happen to me. As hard as it was for me to say, it was equally hard to digest that my God, THE God of us all had allowed something this terrible to happen. I began to question if God even loved me anymore. He couldn't love me if he let this happen. More thoughts had invaded my mind as I started to feed off the enemy's lies because God was silent. Was I wicked? Had I been wicked for shutting out my heart because Craig put Gabriel's head through the wall? I had to ask these questions because I wanted to understand. This offense was constantly on my mind, and as I looked around at the world, I wondered how many people felt the same as I did. This one incident had me questioning God and His intentions for me for a very long time. About three years to be precise. Three years—1,095 days; and I questioned God on each one of them. I had often asked this question because I wanted a definitive answer, and since God had spoken to me when He saved Gabriel's life, I knew it was possible to hear from Him again. All I had to do was listen. Except maybe I wasn't asking the right questions, I told myself.

So many children are going hungry, people dying for no reason it seemed. Ruthless leaders elected into office, and for what? What could the reason possibly be? There were so many people who had no place to lay their head. Millions of people homeless. It was endless. I had begun to wrestle with God our creator and His purpose for our lives. His purpose for our creation. The questions wouldn't stop coming.

In the Bible, David had a moment when he also asked questions. He had done something terribly wrong. He had killed his best friend to cover up a horrible lie. David, a man after God's own heart, committed adultery and murder, and still, God was able to use him.

We are conditioned only to see God and His Love when things are going right. We expect everything to go according to plan, and when things go wrong, we automatically believe that we have done something, or deserve what we are getting. Our consequences have finally caught up with us. Never considering that we live in a fallen world. This place is not our home. It's a constant shuffle of emotions as we tiptoe around our happy, and sad, our scared and angry, and then juggle it with the actual truth. We want to live in this fallen world because it's what we know. It's a short life that has an expiration date, and yet we live it like tomorrow will never end. Too many times we are told, "Go ahead, live your life, who cares what people think, who cares?" In view of this faulty mentality, it is what begins to fuel the wicked mind. Just because you can do something doesn't mean you always should.

Why Do The Wicked Prosper

After having a better understanding of God's love, my next question was, "Why was this wicked person allowed to continue with his life after what he had done to me? Really, God, what is going on?"

Not only did He allow this to happen to me, but now this wicked man was prospering. I had thought about this for some time. Why do the wicked prosper? What is God doing? Why isn't He doing it MY WAY? My thoughts were ultimately getting out of hand. No, I may not be God, BUT isn't the "right thing" to do ultimately the best way to handle this situation? Put him in jail. What if he does this to someone else? What if he is allowed to get away with all of this for several decades? My search again leads me to Job. After Job had a council with his friends and pleaded with God to hear his case, God finally spoke to Job:

Are you the one who has created the heaven and the earth? Job 38

In Job 23:1, Job says

Even today my complaint is bitter; his hand is heavy in spite of my groaning. If only I knew where to find Him; if only I could go to his dwelling! I would state my case before Him and fill my mouth with arguments. I would find out what He would answer me, and consider what He would say.
Job too felt the same way I did. I wanted to sit and talk with God for a little while. My feelings were running the show, and they were in overdrive so much so that I had abandoned all rational thought and lost sight of my foundation. The foundation that God had been forming in my life. Not for one

second had I considered that this was where I was supposed to be. I was too focused on the pain of it all. To focused on the hurt, and too focused on whatever lies the enemy was feeding me at the time. I felt abandoned, and like Job, like David, like Ezekiel, I had stumbled into an area of my life where I honestly did not understand the *who* and *what* and *why* of God. I just felt abandoned, lost, unloved, and alone. Like no one knew how I was feeling, as if I had it all figured out. My feelings were on overload, but my ultimate feeling was that God had left me.

Abandonment

After asking the "why" and "why me" for almost a year, I heard nothing. The old folk talked about grieving the Holy Spirit. And that is precisely what I was doing. "Why me, why me, why me?" Honestly, I don't think I would have been able to hear God because of the state I was in. God very well could have been talking to me, or sending others to comfort me, but in my distress I couldn't hear, feel, or see a thing. I solely focused on my affliction, and ultimately it caused me to become bitter and soon furiously angry with God. Like I even had the right to think in such a way.

In the beginning, I was shocked that it happened, and after that wore off, I was angry that God didn't protect me. However, I never took reflection of myself. It was all God's fault. In my selfish ways, I had somehow become spoiled into thinking that God worked for me. I believed and was led to believe that God was all-loving and all-powerful and beautiful like a rainbow. Never had I been introduced to the side of God that strengthens. The side of God who builds character. The side of God who chastises those He loves. The side of God who will ultimately let you take a road less traveled so that you can choose and see what love looks like. The side of God that will allow you to come back into His loving arms when you are ready. I likened this part of my journey to when I was in junior high, and the teacher told me that Christopher Columbus discovered America. I had accepted that knowledge and carried that information with me all the way to college. Then, when I had arrived at college and delved a little deeper into our US history, I found out that Christopher Columbus didn't discover America, and I felt hoodwinked because the truth was not really the truth anymore. DON'T GET ME WRONG, I was told some truths about God, but I doubt that I was wholly prepared to understand the magnitude of what was going to happen to me. I was not ready for this great offense.

Offenses will come…Luke 17:1-3

Then He said to the disciples, "It is impossible that no offenses will come."

I knew what the Bible said, but the words were not words until I had come to the door and stumbled onto a faith-changing experience that only God and I could navigate together. It was our time. God and I had to travel down a road that I was not prepared for. Still, it was our time. He held my hand, and we walked down another road less traveled.

I have always wanted a deeper relationship with God. At times I prayed, "God don't give up on me. I will get to a time and a place where I will finally understand who You are and what You will be doing for and in my life. Just don't give up on me." Every year I would say to myself, *this is the year I'm going to read the Bible more. This is the year I'm going to go a little deeper with God, and this is the year that I will go to church more.* Except it never happened. Life kept me held hostage by my wants and my so-called needs. So I put God on the back burner until I was ready. Then it came a time when I wasn't ready, because I genuinely wasn't prepared.

This rape had me questioning the God that I loved. The God that if He never did another thing for me, had done more than enough. The God that I was created to serve. This rape had me angry with God because I no longer understood who He was, and what He was, or even why He was anymore. I just knew that I was raped and I no longer trusted God to protect me under any circumstances.

Faith

"Faith is the substance". It had never occurred to me that I had lost faith in God. I had lost all trust in Him; I knew that for sure. My anger and cynicism caused me to remove myself from God. Silly as it may seem, I wanted nothing to do with God. I just wanted to go about my life and do as I pleased, because deep down inside I felt as if God no longer wanted to be a part of my life. Nothing made sense to me anymore, and I so desperately just needed it to make a little sense.

I could understand that I cheated on my husband and these are the consequences of my actions, but what about him putting Gabriel's head through the wall? Should I have drugged him and beat him and broken every bone in his body for what he had done to my child? Should we have just gotten a divorce and ended it all so that we had never reached the point of where he felt the need to rape me? We did stand before God and vow for better or for worse. What about forgiveness? Should we have both forgiven each other and continued to go on with our lives? It may have been an easy fix if we both had - or even one of us had - a better relationship with God. Instead, my relationship with God had suffered a tremendous blow. I no longer wanted to get to know Him anymore because of this. I no longer wanted anything to do with God. I NO LONGER TRUSTED GOD and it no longer mattered to me.

    I had chosen to walk away from God. I was offended by His lack of service to me. As if I could be offended by God. However, I was. I was ushered into a place where God and I were not friends. We stopped talking, and I stopped trusting Him because I could not understand why He allowed this to happen to me. I wanted a life of everything must go right, and nothing should go wrong as long as I TRIED TO LIVE RIGHT and as long as I did my absolute best. Had I considered that my best wasn't good enough? No, not at all. So now I found myself exactly where the devil wanted me to be: out of a relationship with God. God and I were no longer together; we broke up. Only He didn't break up with me. I broke up with Him. I wanted no part of God even if He remotely wanted anything to do with me. Like so many, I blamed God for what these people had done. It was because of whom I chose to associate with, and by nature when something happens to us, we question God because WE have attached ourselves to the wrong people.

Chapter 8

My Relationship With My Heavenly Father

Messed up, because of my Job experience, I already knew I had lost my trust for Him. God had been minimized to a mere man in my eyes because of everything that I was going through. I began to look at Him as if He was a man and His actions were wrong because of how I chose to deal with my circumstances. How would I have wanted to deal with Craig? If it were up to me and my anger, the possibilities would be endless. I no longer trusted God to take care of me as the Bible said. He allowed this to happen and I can no longer trust a God that would do something like this, I began telling myself. However, there was one crucial piece of information that I so comfortably decided to eliminate. I was out of His will. Living my life however I pleased. RIGHTEOUS INDIGNATION, bitterness, and entitlement had already crept in. I stopped talking to God. I stopped praying, and I no longer wanted anything to do with God. "There's no way I can worship a God like this," I told myself. Who would want to worship God? Look at all that has happened. Yes, I'm partly to blame, but so was Craig, and nothing is happening to him. A conversation at an earlier point when our relationship was good had crossed my mind. He had expressed to me that he didn't believe in the Bible. He said the stories couldn't be true because there's no way Adam and Eve could populate the entire world. He also said it was unlikely that some of the other stories existed. He didn't even believe, but I did. In my mind, I now thought that God was protecting him and not me. I believed in God, and he didn't. So why are you protecting him and not me? The next series of questions hurt and I can't help but give place to the enemy once more. The thoughts devoured my reality, and I accepted them, saddened and disconnected once again.

    I knew that my relationship with God was slowly deteriorating. It hurt too much to continue worshipping Him after everything. Not only did he not protect me, but He also had all power and just did nothing. That hurt most of all.

"Our Lord is great and very powerful. There is no limit to what he knows." Psalm 147:5.

Knowing this, the fire that I once had and the hunger to get to know God had been extinguished. The pain was unbearable, and it was all I could focus on. How dare God. How dare He allow me to have to go down this road. I had been a good Christian. In my mind, I had tried my absolute best to do the right thing, but just like everyone else, I had made a couple of mistakes. We all make bad decisions. Ultimately, my heart was in the right place, I thought. So I felt that God was wrong. He had gotten it wrong. I didn't deserve this assault. I didn't deserve to have my heart broken. Craig cast the first stone by putting Gabriel's head through a wall, and now these are the consequences of his actions. Husbands, love your wives as you love yourself. That's what it says in the Bible. He got it all wrong. Maybe he misread that part in Ephesians 5:25. He should have known that something like this would have killed me. Craig's actions put a huge wedge in our relationship. How was I supposed to overlook him, his actions, and what he did to Gabriel? It scared me more than anything. In my mind, it was going to happen again, and it was only a matter of time before it happened to me, or one of the other children. I merely declined his offer to become an accomplice to his crime. I've seen too many mothers, too many times, going to jail because they knew of the abuse and didn't report it to the proper authorities. Mothers simply not doing anything to help their children, thereby causing further irrevocable damage, and later on, this damage manifesting itself in different ways.

I had found myself at a crossroads, and it seemed to creep up on me and slap me in the face. How was I going to move forward with God? Was it even possible to repair? Lots of times, I was told that God wants to have a relationship with us. God wants a personal relationship with us. Not just a one day a week Sunday type of relationship with us. Except, the storm that He allowed had caused my distrust. More questions fueled my mistrust:

Does God want a relationship with me?

Why would He allow something like this?

Does God even care?

Do I even know who God is?

Is there even a God?

In the beginning, I knew God desires to have a relationship with us, and I had to ask myself once more, "How can you possibly have a relationship with the Heavenly Father, if you know nothing about Him?" Nothing about what He has done for you and nothing about what He wants for your life. At this point in time, it no longer mattered to me. I was still angry. I was still deeply hurt that God didn't save me from this terrible incident. Deep down I no longer wanted to care. Maybe this was how things were supposed to be. This was the fate of my life.

Church was a thing of the past for me. I kept myself at home, and in isolation—exactly where the enemy wanted me to be. There was no need to try and pretend that this was where I wanted to be, even though I knew I needed to be there. After a long conversation and many, many tears, Chris pleaded with me to go to church. It had been a long time since I had gone because God and I were still not talking, but to appease Chris, I gave in. "What harm could it do?" I thought. He knew how I felt, and just to make him happy, I went. On this particular Sunday, the preacher Reverend Lyde preached a sermon on, "You Are Special!" It felt as if he was talking directly to me. I was not prepared for that one.

The circumstances of my new normal had me preparing myself. I was preparing myself to continue life without God. I had it all figured out; God didn't love me, He wanted nothing to do with me because he allowed Craig to rape me, and there was no longer any trust. Trust was a thing of the past. Little did I know that God had other plans, of course.

When I was younger, I knew after you accepted Jesus Christ as your Lord and Savior, you were taking a small step in the right direction. You recognize that you need God to live a better and more productive life. You make a conscious decision to want to change the way you live, and you want to turn your life around. Now, none of this happens overnight. Believe me; I tried my very best to live right. I tried my best not to lie, not to cheat, or steal. I tried MY best to do everything that I thought God wanted me to do. With the commandments as my guide, I accepted the covenant and said to myself that this was all I had to do. I made two crucial mistakes at that time.

Number one, I concluded that that was all I needed to do to live a better more productive life, and two, nothing would happen to me because I had accepted Jesus Christ as my Lord and Savior, so I was covered. I couldn't have been further from the truth. In spite of my tantrum and not wanting anything to do with God, I couldn't stay away. There was still a longing to understand why things happened the way that they did, and a hunger to be in His presence. Someone had to be blamed, and I was not so easily swayed that it was me. Just like that, I found myself sitting in church waiting for the preacher to help me understand.

"I WONDER IF THERE IS ANYBODY IN HERE TODAY, WHO IS NOT ASHAMED TO TESTIFY, THAT GOD KEPT YOU ALIVE WHEN YOU WERE IN A WEAKENED CONDITION! YOU OUGHT GO ON AND TESTIFY! TELL SOMEBODY, 'GOD KEPT ME ALIVE!' GOD KEPT YOU FROM OPPORTUNISTIC ENTITIES THAT WANTED TO CAPITALIZE ON YOUR VULNERABILITY," his words, loud and boisterous.

The congregation shouting, "Preach Reverend," as I sit watching and waiting to see where his sermon is going.

WHY DID HE DO IT? HE DID IT BECAUSE YOU MATTER! HE DID IT BECAUSE YOU ARE SOMEBODY TO HIM! HE DID IT BECAUSE YOU'RE IMPORTANT! HE DID IT BECAUSE YOU ARE SIGNIFICANT! HE DID IT BECAUSE YOU HAVE PURPOSE! HE DID IT BECAUSE YOU HAVE PURPOSE! HE DID IT BECAUSE HE AIN'T THROUGH WITH YOU YET! HE DID IT BECAUSE THERE IS RHYME AND REASON TO YOUR LIFE! IF YOU EVER AGAIN DOUBT YOUR IMPORTANCE OR YOUR VALUE; ALL YOU HAVE TO DO IS LOOK BACK OVER YOUR SHOULDER AND SEE WHAT GOD HAS ALREADY BROUGHT YOU THROUGH AND KEPT YOU FROM!

In my mind this all pertained to me, but as he kept going I began to realize Craig could have also staked his claim to these same exact words. His life still mattered. He still mattered to God.

The preacher was talking of a battle in 1 Samuel 30 between David and the Amalekites. At first, David and his 600 loyal men were scheduled to fight in a battle alongside King Achish, but

Philistia's leaders did not want David to fight with them. They believed David would turn on them in battle. So after traveling for three days, they were told to go back home. When they arrived back home, they had been attacked by the Amalekites. Their village burned, and all possessions taken along with their wives and children. The men were very angry with David, and there was talk of them wanting to stone him. These men had been loyal to David through all his trouble, and they were angry with him because he had taken them on a long march to a battle that had not been fought, only to come back to their homes burned to the ground. They had left their families vulnerable to attack while being loyal to David. Of course, David understood their anger, grief, and their wounded hearts. Soon David inquired of the Lord as to what he should do:

> *Then David said to Abiathar the priest, Ahimelech's son, "Please bring the ephod here to me." And Abiathar brought the ephod to David. So David inquired of the Lord, saying, "Shall I pursue this troop? Shall I over-take them?"* 1 Samuel 30:7-8

Now David, after hearing from God that he should pursue the Amalekites and would recover all, set out on a journey to find his wife and children. Upon the search for the robbers who had taken their wives and children, David and his men stumbled on an Egyptian man who was lying unconscious in the desert. He was a slave who had been tossed aside by his master because he was too sick to travel on. David and his men cared for this Egyptian slave. They gave him bread, water, and fruit. Because of their generosity and kindness, the slave recovered. Soon David realized that this man was important. He was useful. This man mattered to God and David. This man led David and his men to the camp of the robbers who had taken their wives and children to enslave them. This man was valuable.

> "I'M STILL VALUABLE TO GOD!" SEE, I MIGHT NOT BE VALUABLE TO YOU BUT I AM STILL VALUABLE TO GOD! HOW VALUABLE ARE YOU? YOU ARE VALUABLE ENOUGH FOR GOD TO STILL WAKE YOU UP IN THE MORNING"

Again the preacher's words echo in the church, and I sit. The hurt begins to suffocate me. All the pain I had been thinking about on the way to church as well as the previous years had me stuck. I couldn't move forward with my life, and I couldn't stop thinking about it. All I could do was cry. I immediately start to think of Craig. The flood gates open and it feels as if I am drowning yet again in my tears, all while everyone is standing praising and shouting "Hallelujah!" I'm sitting practically in the middle of the church bawling, and I'm angry. Over and over each scene plays in my mind. They remain on constant repeat. I want to scream with all my might, "WHY!" Why does he get to be special? Why? After all he did, how does he still get to be special? This is unreal! Tears continue to roll down my cheeks. This is not fair. He gets to do what he wants, gets away with it, and he's still special!

No! God! No!

I'm more than mad because the preacher explains that we are all special to God. From the tallest to the shortest, big-boned, skinny, meek, or broken-hearted. The murderer, the loved, and the lost are all special to God. We are all a part of an intricate web of fine detail that only God can navigate to get us to our expected end. Angry as I was, I couldn't fathom that this man would still be special in the eyes of God.

All these feelings and emotions came rushing back, AGAIN! I'm in church, and my anger shuts out my ability to listen any further. The enemy starts speaking to me.

This is ridiculous!

He rapes you, and God loves him anyway?

Craig is more special than you, and you're serving God anyway.

You know what you have to do.

I know what you should do.

You should go ahead and kill him and let him go home to meet his maker.

Why are you still sitting there?

The devil wasn't supposed to be able to distract me and take away the word from me in church, but he did. Now I understood what the old folks were talking about when they said, "The devil goes to church faithfully every Sunday."
I stand to my feet to come out of the pew because I want to go to the car and wait until church is over. Chris looks at me and asks what's wrong.

He sees me crying, and he knows what's wrong, because crying was all I did. So without a doubt, I know he already knew what it was. I tell him I can't listen anymore and that I need to go to the car. He grabs me, and he won't let me go. He sits me down, wraps his arms around me, dries my eyes with a tissue and holds me for the duration of the service.

It vexed me that after all that had been done, Craig was still special in God's eyes. It irritated me to my core that God didn't see him as I did. He was a murderer and a rapist. It didn't matter that Craig put Gabriel's head through the wall. He was still special. No matter what he had done, or was about to do in this life, he would still be considered special, and that hurt me. That cut me all the way to the white meat. I began to think to myself, *How is this possible?* On the ride home, I told myself that it was time to take matters into my own hands. God was taking too long to set him straight. It was going to be ok; I knew my children were going to be ok, and I thought to myself that maybe jail wouldn't be that bad. No sooner had I thought this than God began to speak to me.

Your ways are not My ways.

When you were out there doing whatever it was you wanted to do with Sinister, you never considered the consequences of your actions, nor did it bother you. Now you want me to rush and fix this situation.

I waited for you, and now you must wait for Me.

Yes, he is still special because all things work for My good.

With tears in my eyes, I knew that God was right. I never considered my consequences. There's a lump in my throat. I just wanted to be happy, so I decided to do it. I couldn't even consider my children and the impact that a divorce would forever imprint on their lives, because I was too selfish to allow God to fix Craig. Had I taken a moment to think instead of reacting, maybe we could have been in a better place. All I wanted to do at the time was respond to the hurt he inflicted on me. I didn't want to take the time to pray and ask God to fight on my behalf. I wanted that quick fix - the easy way out - and my flesh chose Sinister.

I was mad because God was right, and mad because I knew that I had a very long road ahead of me. I had to wait on the Lord. Wait on the Lord: Be of good courage, and he shall strengthen thine heart; wait, I say, on the Lord. Psalm 27:14

I finally began to pray, even though I didn't want to.

Lord, I don't know how to wait. I'm angry that you have not done anything to help me with this situation. I don't see anything happening, and I don't trust that you are working on my behalf. Honestly, I don't want to wait, because I don't know how. Help me, Lord! Help me to wait for you, Lord!

After saying that prayer, I didn't feel any better, but it was I that had turned my back on him, and not that God didn't want to hear me. Everything that I had learned about God, I chose to toss away in the evening's trash. The foundation had been laid, and I had decided to throw it all away as if I had to start all over again.

Train up a child in the way they should go... Proverbs 22:6

Because of this offense, I had begun to forget what God had done for me. Not just today in church, but every day. I had so comfortably forgotten to take inventory of the good things that God had done for my family and me. I could see how all the other details made sense, whether good or bad. However, I couldn't understand how this one thing that only God knew I had hidden in my heart could be part of His divine plan. It couldn't possibly make any sense to me. I began looking in the cracks of my mind to try and figure out what it all could likely mean. Why had this been allowed? A God as powerful as the Bible says, saw and knew this was coming. I was the only one blindsided.

As we drive home from church, I begin to wonder what this is all about. There must be a reason, there must be a purpose in my pain, and I needed to go to God and find out. My mind is drawn to a sermon in which Joyce Meyers was speaking about her life and the trauma she had to endure at the hands of her father. Being sexually abused for years and not even her mother saved her from his abuse. Somehow, she made it. Not only did she make it, but in her later years before her father died, she was able to forgive him and help him in any way she could. WOW! She wasn't ruined, her life didn't end, and she had become successful.

Suddenly, it hit me. Enlightened once more, I believed God and the devil were playing games. I elected to take another ride on the rollercoaster of my emotions once more, and a fire had been lit yet again. My emotions were running the show, and I chose to think on any thought that came to mind. I gave attention to it quickly, and not only that, but I also believed it. That seemed like the best explanation I could come up with at the time. Quite possibly, God was using the devil to scare everyone into submission. That's why He didn't help me. Pain has a way of making you completely lose your mind, and now my mind was blown. My pain was intense. I found myself asking God more questions:

Why create us to play these head games, Lord?

Why not just destroy the devil and get it over with?

Why continue to allow such destruction in the world?

God, what's with all these games?

I was still angry and had not concluded that my anger was keeping me away from God. For some reason, I wanted to continue to blame God for all the things that had happened to me. Anger crept up on me once more, and I found myself focusing on the pain. It seemed like it was impossible to let go of.

The Games God is Playing

Subsequently, in my anger, I had gotten to the point where I concluded that God was playing games. I was so angry that I thought God was playing games. I remember speaking to Chris saying, "I want no part of this!" This is a game that God and the devil are playing, and we are the chess pieces. Pawns in an intricate game of wits, skill, and strategy. Whose turn would it be to shuffle me around? Was it the devil's as destruction falls, or God's as He enlightens and brings joy? Was it the devil who would bring about this destruction, so that God would get the glory as He picks up the broken pieces of our lives? Why play these games?

It was at that time that I finally realized how uneducated I was as to who God is. Early on, I had learned that God was a protector with Gabriel when He saved him from an early appointment with the bumper and wheels of my car. Somehow, that same protection didn't apply to me. Since I was now left staring at myself in the mirror wondering who God was, protector was no longer in my vocabulary.

Somehow it had lost its true meaning because I was left rationalizing what I had done to warrant such punishment. Where had I gone wrong? The fact that Craig was not getting punished was no longer on my mind. My focus was solely on my actions and the unexpected outcome. It was important for me to understand the God I had served once more.

I stumbled on the Book of Job to the passage where God and the devil were having a conversation.

One day the angels came to present themselves before the Lord, and Satan also came with them. The Lord said to Satan, "Where have you come from?"
Satan answered the Lord, "From roaming through the earth and going back and forth in it." Then the Lord said to Satan, "Have you considered my servant Job? There is no one on earth like him; he is blameless and upright, a man who fears God and shuns evil." Job 1:6-8

Without studying the passage, and looking at it with definite superficiality, I had concluded that it was here that the games had begun. God and the devil are playing games with people's lives. God is offering up his servant Job to be tormented by the devil. A man that God himself says is blameless and upright. As I continue my investigation, the devil concludes that the only reason Job fears God is that God is protecting him and his wealth. Without going deeper, I easily came to this conclusion.

"Does Job fear God for nothing?" Satan replied. "Have you not put a hedge around him and his household and everything he has? You have blessed the work of his hands so that his flocks and herds are spread throughout the land. But stretch out your hand and strike everything he has, and he will surely curse you to your face." Job 1:9-11

God loved Job, and He still allowed the devil to torment him. He offered him up like fresh meat brought to slaughter. My thoughts trap me exactly where I needed to be. Mesmerized by the implication of a righteous man, it was hard to let that passage go. It meant so much, but still offered me so little because I was not able to understand. I had to go deeper with God. I want to fight the need to understand, but this part of the Bible had me at "Hello!" I mean like really, "Hello God, what is going on?" How is it possible that a loving and caring God would send the devil to torment one of his blameless servants? Job offered up sacrifices daily to the Lord for his children just in case they might have sinned. Every day, this man worshipped the Lord. Job loved the Lord and did his best to live the right way, and God allowed the great deceiver to go after him. He didn't even have a moment to prepare. Job lost everything in a day. One day—all that he had was gone. One after the other, his servants came and witnessed what they had seen and heard.

So now I'm left wondering how my God is a good God. Little did I know that the answer to my "How and why...why me?" question could be found in this exact passage.

"Does Job fear God for nothing?" Satan replied. "Have you not put a hedge around him and his household and everything he has? You have blessed the work of his hands so that his flocks and herds are spread throughout the land. But stretch out your hand and strike everything he has, and he will surely curse you to your face." Job 1:9-11

The Lord said to Satan, "Very well, then, everything he has is in your power, but on the man himself do not lay a finger." Then Satan went out from the presence of the Lord. Job 1:12

Again, at the beginning of my walk with God, I was always told that we Christians have been given a choice. A simple choice to choose God, or not choose God. Choose whether you believe in God and what He stands for, or not to believe. Your choice ultimately belongs to you, of course, but it is a choice, nonetheless. Simple yet profound, and the fact of making a decision was presented to us, to enlighten. This same choice would have no meaning if God removed the ability to choose. I had to consider this. Had God said to us all, "Follow me, love me, pick me because you have no choice," then I could understand how some people could call Him fake. I could understand their side. A God who makes you follow Him and punishes you for it. However, the truth is, you don't have to believe in God. You don't have to believe in the Bible, and you don't have to believe in eternal life. You can live the way you want, take as much revenge as you want, and ultimately be whomever you want to be. That is your choice if that is what you choose.

My heart hardened like Pharaoh. It was all I knew how to do at that time. It was the defense mechanism I had grown to accept and use to build myself back up. It was what I used to protect myself. God says in the Bible that the sun shines on the just and the unjust alike. Matthew 5:45. So the wicked and the good people of this world receive the same treatment from God. They receive the same love and the same chastisement. I had to visit the Bible once more and look at what and who it says God is. Everything in me wanted to stay where I was, but I was only bitter and angry. In my heart, I was becoming more and more isolated and still hurt because of my new epiphany.

Who Is God

We believe the scriptures teach that there is one and only one living and true God; an infinite, intelligent spirit whose name is Jehovah, the maker and supreme ruler of heaven and earth. Inexpressibly glorious in holiness and worthy of all possible honor, confidence and love, that in the unity of the Godhead there are three persons: the Father, the Son, and the Holy Ghost. Equal in every divine perfection and execution, but distinct yet harmonious offices in the great work of redemption. This is an article of faith, in reference to the true God. As Christians, this is our core belief system.

I have learned that God is many things to many people. To some who are suffering, God is nothing, non-existent, mean, and unkind. Some even believe that God is waiting to punish us for everything that we do. Whatever we are going through at the moment seems to be who God is for us at the time. If God is protecting us, then we see Him as our protector. If He keeps us from all hurt, harm, and danger, then God is awesome. If we cannot feel His presence, then He has abandoned us. The world shapes our view of who God is as we go through our trials, our troubles, and our hurts. It also shapes our view as we go through happiness and our good times.

    Feeding solely off of my emotions, and what I believed, my flawed sense of God caused me to begin to think that I had always been abandoned. I had never gone through anything that made me question my existence, and now I was face to face with this trouble. It was time to get to the heart of the matter. I sat like Job in my dirt; no sores, I had not even lost my family or any of my possessions. However, I could relate. I lost myself. In no way were our situations identical, but the pain was just as intense for me.

    Job, in the Bible, sat and listened as his friends begin to tell him that he had done something wrong. His actions somehow caused God to punish him in such a way, because God would not allow him to suffer if he hadn't done something wrong. Jobs friends even concluded that God had permitted the suffering so that it would turn believers away from wickedness and keep us from sinning. In John 9:2, it states, "Rabbi, his disciples asked him, why was this man born blind? Was it because of his own sins or his parent's sins?" Jesus answered simply, "It was neither, this happened so that the power of God can be seen in him."

    Now I sit forced to see God for who He is. I'm now left considering three things. Had God chastised me for not ending this relationship? Had God allowed this because He wanted to get the glory? Had this been the order of my steps whether I was righteous or not? Regardless of any road I had chosen, I found myself here in the middle of my mess, looking for someone to blame, and it was God for allowing this trouble my way.

    I allowed the world view to sculpt my thoughts as I envisioned God to be angry with me for it all, and now it was time to be corrected and retrained - a thought that had jumped in my mind on several occasions. Now, who is God? Not who is God to me, but who is God? The Bible tells us that:

God is spirit - God is Spirit, and those who worship Him must worship in spirit and truth. John 4:24

God is Love - He who does not love does not know God, for God is love. 1 John 4:8

God is the Alpha and Omega - I am the Alpha and the Omega, the Beginning and the End, the First and the Last. Revelation 22:13

God is not a liar - In hope of eternal life which God, who cannot lie, promised before time began. Titus 1:2

God is faithful - He is the Rock, his work is perfect; For all His ways are justice, a God of truth and without injustice; Righteous and upright. Deuteronomy 32:4

God is our creator - In the beginning God created the heavens and the earth. Genesis 1:1

God is merciful - For the Lord your God is merciful, He will not forsake you nor destroy you, nor forget the covenant of your fathers which He swore to them. Deuteronomy 4:31

God is the Word - In the beginning was the Word, and the Word was with God, and the Word was God. John 1:1

God is light - The Lord is my light and my salvation; Whom shall I fear? The Lord is the strength of my life; of whom shall I be afraid. Psalm 27:1

God is our strength - I can do all things through Christ who strengthens me. Philippians 4:13

God is good - Oh taste and see that the Lord is good; Blessed is the man who trusts in Him! Psalm 34:8

God is mighty - The Lord your God in your midst, the Mighty One, will save; He will rejoice over you with gladness, He will quiet you with His love, He will rejoice over you with singing. Zephaniah 3:17

God is rich in mercy - But God, who is rich in mercy, because of His great love with which He loved us, even when we were dead in trespasses, made us alive together with Christ (by grace you have been saved). Ephesians 2:4-6

God is righteous - For the Lord is righteous, He loves righteousness; His countenance beholds the upright. Psalm 11:7

God is faithful - If we confess our sins, He is faithful and just to forgive us our sins and to cleanse us from all unrighteousness. 1 John 1:9

God is everlasting - Have you not known? Have you not heard? The everlasting God, the Lord, the Creator of the ends of the earth, neither faints nor is weary. His understanding is unsearchable. He gives power to the weak, and to those who have no might, He increases strength. Isaiah 40:28-29

    For this reason, after taking the time to search and see for myself, it would be beyond me to pick and choose what I want to believe. Should I take the good out of the Bible and leave the rest? I had wanted to at a certain point in my life because of my modest understanding of God and His love for me. It was not until I sought God did I see Him for myself in spite of my circumstances. After speculating and questioning God for so long, as well as what I assumed others would reason, I finally recognized the God I serve, and not the God I learned to serve.

    After searching for such a long time, I had to ask myself, how can I look at God and say He was not fair to allow this? If He wanted to be fair, there was so much more that I deserved than what had happened over the course of my lifetime. If God wanted to be fair, I could and should only look at this one way; I don't deserve salvation, and I don't deserve to go to heaven because of all the things I have done. Some of the things I have locked away that no one knows but me. The things I plan to take to my grave. If God just allowed some of the things to happen to me that I do deserve, I'd probably not be able to take it. No, God is sovereign, and I had the nerve to question my Creator - on more than one occasion might I add. I had to finally accept that He knows the way that I should take, He knows the amount of pressure to apply to get me to my expected end, and He knows me.

Chapter 9

Lord Help Me

Finally, I had to ask God for help. I was ashamed and embarrassed. Ashamed, because of my feelings. Embarrassed because of what happened to me, and even more uneasy because there was nothing I could do about my circumstances. Crippled by the thoughts in my mind, I had finally come to terms with myself. There was no need to hold on to this anger any longer. Baffled as to the exact route that I needed to take, I thought it was best to get professional help. I was going in circles, and my heart couldn't take any more of this crazy rollercoaster that I had elected to stay on. I wanted off. For my sanity and the sake of my children, I needed to reach out and grab hold of anything that would help me stand. I needed to get back to where I was. I wasn't even sure I could get back to who I once was, but I finally wanted to try.

It was time to forgive God, to let go of all the hurt and do my best to take the next step further in any direction. I had been in the same spot for so long that I had forgotten what it was like to do anything. To be proactive in my own life. To love life, or even want to see the sunset that was once on my bucket list. My days had been consumed with wanting to know the details of everything, and I couldn't see past the worst part of it all. Sure, this tragic thing happened to me, but I'm here. Dear God, I'm here, and I'm alive. He could very well have protected me when I had lost my breath, and it felt as if I could not breathe. God could have also spoken it into existence, and that breath I had taken when his hands were around my throat could have been my last. In the blink of an eye, I could have been standing before my Heavenly Father on the day of judgment giving an account of my life. No, it was finally time to get myself together. This man could no longer have any control over me. I had to take it all back. It was wrong that I had given Craig this much thought and time covering myself in so much hurt. I had been robbing myself of a good life, by relinquishing my power to the pain of not knowing as I trapped myself in my mind, continually playing the details over and over. Constantly asking the who, what, where, when, and why.

Finally, I had to let it all go, but I had no idea how.

A trip on the web helped me come across a doctor whom I wanted to try and bare my soul with to help me dig myself out of the pit that I had stumbled into. She was a psychologist as well as a life coach. My insides were unsure of her ability to help someone like me. I had assumed that I was just a bit too far gone. However, I was determined to find the help that I needed, and as hard as it was, I had to put one foot in front of the other to try and fix me.

Dr. Rodriguez's office wasn't too far from where I lived. A ten-minute drive was all I could stand at the moment. Her office was on the other side of town which was close enough for me. So I placed a call to make an appointment, but the call went to voicemail. I hated leaving messages. Unfortunately, I had to if I was going to speak with her.

"Hello, my name is Denise, and I'd like to make an appointment. If you could kindly give me a call back at 555-2121 I would appreciate it. That's 555-2121. Thank you, speak to you soon."

I hung up the phone and then waited. Patience had never been one of my best qualities, but I knew she would call back, so I figured I wouldn't have to wait that long, and as soon as that thought came to me, the phone rang, "Hello, this is Dr. Rodriguez. I got your message. I do apologize, I was on another call. How may I help you?" I then explain - not in so many words - that I would like to sit down and talk with her. She says ok and gives me an appointment for the end of the week. Relieved, I take a deep breath, say thank you, and hang up the phone. No sooner had the call ended than the tears begin to flow. Tears of joy were rolling down my cheeks because that was a big step for me. Still a little traumatized from my hospital visit, I wasn't sure she was going to believe me. I'm still not sure she does, but at least she was willing to talk about it, and that's what I told myself.

Back when all of this happened, I told myself I had to go to the hospital. I had finally gotten the nerve and the strength to go to the hospital to get checked out. I was scared, and I thought to myself if I report this, he will probably get angry and come back and do it again. "Good! I don't care anymore," I told myself. "I don't care what he does. If something else happens, then at least it will all be on record, and he would be a person of interest."

Upon entry into the emergency room, I figured it would be a long wait; however, there wasn't anyone in the waiting room. *Great! Just my luck*, I say in my inside voice. I'm torn between walking into the waiting room any further, or turning around and going back home. Reluctantly, I go to the window and give my name and insurance information to the woman sitting behind the desk before I proceed to find a spot to sit in the empty waiting room. "I don't want to be here. I don't want to be here," I tell myself. All I kept thinking was that these people are not going to believe me. Just as I sat down, I hear my name being called from a room about 5 feet away from the front desk. I go inside the room, and the woman looks at me through a pair of glasses too thin for her face. Her hair in a ponytail, with her dark blue scrubs on, she seems pleasant, almost caring, and with a small dash of concern. "How may I help you?" she asks.

I take a deep breath, and I tell her I've been drugged and raped.

"How may I help you?" she asks again. I looked at her confused and realize that I had not said a word. So I take another deep breath, and it almost seems as if I said it in slow motion.

"I have been drugged and raped." The words don't seem real, and by the look on her face I see that she heard me this time. Her eyes got a little wider than before and she says, "Ok, wait here one moment." What almost seemed like forever was probably only a few minutes, and she steps back into the room. "We have a room for you," she softly announces. I'm scared to move, and my body feels stiff. It's a struggle to move, and I feel like I'm a deer caught in headlights. I don't want to go anywhere. The nurse ushers me through a corridor, down a hallway, and past four doors to a large room. Every door is closed, and then I remember that I am the only one in the hospital at the moment. It's so quiet in the emergency room; no monitors beeping, no screaming for help, and no one crying. Not even a television showing the morning's soap opera. Each step felt like I was walking the green mile, as new faces behind the large desk in the middle of the room look on at me with pity in their eyes. Had my dilemma spread already through the bowels of the emergency room that fast? It had only been seconds.

A nurse comes in and asks me if I would be comfortable waiting with someone, and I say ok. I wanted to say no, but the truth is, I didn't want to be there by myself. "I'll call someone for you," she says. Not sure of the procedure, I say ok. I just wanted it all to be over, but I knew the tests had to be done. Seconds turned into minutes, and minutes into almost what seemed like a half hour, and she walks in. A tall, thin woman with blonde hair. Her clothes reminded me of the '60s, as if she was stuck in a time warp. She looks to be in her early 50s. Her voice is soft, and she begins to talk to me in almost a whisper.

"How are you?" she asks.

I tell her that I'm fine, my face unable to hide my disdain for her dumb question.

She begins to tell me who she is, which agency she is from, and how they will be able to help me. Then she gives me a bit of her background. She tells me that she too had been raped. I'm left wondering if she is telling the truth, or possibly trying to get me to feel more at ease with her as she begins to question me about my rape.

"Can you tell me what happened?" still with the same soft voice.

I begin to tell her everything that I remember, and she sits quietly as I regurgitate all the dates, times, and my feelings on her. The tears begin to flow. I was so mad that I was standing there crying. I wanted to be stronger than I was, but they wouldn't stop. The more I talked, the more I cried. She didn't try to hug me, or even tell me it was going to be all right; she just sat there and listened.

"We have to report this," she said, "Do you want to make a report?"

"Yes, it needs to be done," I said.

"One moment," she says and disappears out of the room. The next time she comes back into the room she has an officer with her. My heart is pounding. It feels as if it's about to jump out of my chest. I look at him. I want to hurry up and tell him what happened because I feel so stupid. How could I have let this happen to me?

"Hello," he says.

"Hello," I reply.

He's tall with blonde hair slicked back with a lot of gel. He has the face of a model. Chiseled, perfect features, and ice cold blue eyes. "Can you please tell me what happened?" he asks. I don't want to explain what happened again, but I knew I had to. As I begin to tell him, he pulls a pad of paper from his back pocket. He takes the pen from his front shirt pocket, looks at me and starts to write, then lets out a long sigh. His uniform is spotless. Everything is in place, not even a piece of lint anywhere.

"Mum hmmm, ok. Can I please ask you a question?"

"Yes, sure."

"Have you had any headaches lately?"

"Yes, I have."

"Have you been tested recently for your headaches?"

"No, I haven't," I tell him.

"Well, I think you need to possibly have a CAT scan because there might be some underlying problems that we don't know of."

I knew what he was trying to imply. Instead of just taking the report, he felt the need to give me his opinion. What he said hurt me even more, and it was at that time I realized why more women don't come forward when they are raped. Mostly, because of cops like him. Instead of just taking the report, he had suddenly transformed into a doctor and was able to diagnose patients. My heart was heavy. I just wanted to shut down and get out of there as fast as I could. I didn't even want to finish the exam. To me there was no reason, because they somehow had their minds made up already. He didn't believe me. He implied that there was something wrong with my brain, and I needed to have it checked to see if what I said happened, actually happened.

The blonde woman excuses herself from the room and asks the officer if she could speak to him outside. She can see the change in my demeanor. As she leaves, the doctor comes in the room. He seems agitated.

"What is going on?" He's annoyed. "Why isn't she on the table?" He lets out a sigh and walks out of the room. I begin to look around for the cameras. I must be in the twilight zone. What is going on here, I ask myself? I put my head in my hands and cry, a loud hard cry and I want to scream. I can't stay any longer. All I want to do is leave. I'm not concerned about finding out what is going on with me any longer. I just want to leave the hospital.

I look around for my clothes, walk to the chair I placed them on and begin to get dressed. The nurse looks at me and asks where I'm going. Quickly, I tell her that I'm leaving.

"Please don't leave without doing the exam." The blonde woman knocks and re-enters the room as I am telling the ER nurse I'm leaving.

"I don't care about the exam anymore," I tell her. "What is wrong with you people? What is wrong with that doctor? He's angry because I'm not spread eagle on the table ready for him considering the situation. No, I have to leave!"

"Please, we can get you another doctor! Just wait. Please!" Both the blonde woman and the ER nurse plead with me not to go. I put on my clothes without saying another word, and I walk out of the hospital with my head in my hands, crying and ashamed. How could they treat people like that?

Why would they want to treat people like that? God, why do people like this exist? I'm left feeling empty, and now I'll never know what happened, and he will never be held accountable. I drove home brokenhearted once more.

Next week seemed to come flying around the corner. I ring the bell to the therapist's front door hoping that she won't be there, wishing that she might have had an emergency and she had to leave unexpectedly to visit another patient. It's even harder now to tell people what happened to me because of my hospital visit. Even if she didn't believe me, she had to sit there and listen because I was paying her to. Just my luck, she answers the door. I want to run away, but it seems like my feet are glued to the front steps. "Come in," she says.

I enter, and instantly I am met with a warm feeling. Pictures of her children align the walls and lead into the kitchen. Earth tones cover the walls. The foyer was red, and into the living room the color changes to a warm beige. It makes me feel at ease. She asks me to follow her into her office. She opens a door and green hugs the walls, and the first thing I notice is a large wood bookcase. It's filled with books, of course, but what catches my eye is more pictures of her family. She had two boys.

"Have a seat on the couch if you'd like," she says.

I sit and begin to scan the room; anything to take my mind off of what is about to happen. I'm nervous. It's the hospital visit and the police officer that has the words trapped in my throat. I'm not even sure I want to say it. However, I know that I need to do something before it's too late. The pain had been all I could think about, and the mental stress and draining thoughts had me wanting the end to come sooner than later. I didn't really want to die. I was just tired of the pain. Tired of the thoughts that wouldn't end. They were so hard to deal with, and I didn't know how to just shut it all down so that I could get a break. I didn't know how to deal with the stress of the rape, or the thoughts that bombarded me every single day.

"So, what brings you to my office?" Rodriguez asks. I breathe a long sigh. I'm not sure where to begin. "At the beginning, that's always best," Dr. Rodrigues flashes a smile. I look at her, and I'm not sure I should trust her. I just met her, and she already wants me to pour out my soul. We sit in silence for a moment, and then I begin to tell her.

"I was raped," I begin.

"How did this happen?" she asks.

Right after I tell her, the tears begin to fall again. I don't want to cry anymore, not even one tear. I've spent too many years crying over this, but I can't help it. These new tears I cried were more of a release, and I knew this was a part of the process. Talking about what happened to me was going to be the beginning of my healing, I told myself. She sat and listened to me, and I kept talking and crying.

"This is more common than you think. I have a friend that told me of this exact thing. There are so many household items that can be used to render a person incapacitated. I'm going to talk with her, find out what they are, and I want you to look around your house and let me know if these items are there," she says. I shake my head in disbelief. Her words keep ringing in my head. She said it was "common". It lightened the load of despair, but the fact that it happened still caused an enormous amount of anxiety. However, it felt better to finally talk with someone. I wasn't sure how this all was going to go, but my exhaustion caused me to reevaluate the next step I was going to take, and finally I accepted the need to speak with someone. So many things were happening, and I felt like my life was spiraling out of control. She began to ask me to tell her a little about the events that led up to Craig feeling the need to drug me. Where did we meet? How long were we dating? Do we have any children together? Each question took me back to the beginning when things were good with us. "Of course, we had problems like anyone else, but things were good until he lost his job," I explained to her.

Her next series of questions caught me off guard. She began to ask me what type of relationship I had with my father. I wasn't sure how to answer the question because I didn't understand, and I wanted so much to know why the questions about my family had anything to do with my father and lack thereof. It must have shown on my face because she began to help me understand where she was going. "You see, people have a hard time understanding God because they take the human experience and relate to God in the same way," she explains. "So if you had, or are having a difficult relationship with your father, you will, in turn, have a bad relationship with God. If the father that God gave to protect, guide and direct us doesn't do any of those things, we might have a hard time separating the two," she further explains. Now, my relationship with my father had not always been a good one, but I believed that we were a work in progress. The therapist also simplified not having a solid foundation with my earthly father caused more trouble with my heavenly Father. So the trouble I was having, and feeling at the moment was a combination. She also explained, "I had not thought that God wasn't going to help me through this hurt because I had issues with my earthly father." It wasn't until she unfolded my hurt and mistrust that I was able to sit back and think, "Could this woman be right?" This was a question that I had to sleep on.

Suddenly our time was up, and I made an appointment to speak with her the following week. As I left her office, it felt as if a significant weight had been lifted off of me. I felt lighter, and it felt so good. It had been so long that I had felt this way, and I had no idea what to make of it, except that I liked it. When I was initially raped, I wanted to try to go to one of those groups to fight my way back to some type of normalcy, but I couldn't bring myself to go. My trouble with going to the group was that I knew I would have felt uncomfortable sitting there. That was just my insecurity shutting myself out of getting help any sooner. I tried looking on the internet, but I couldn't even put one foot in front of the other to go. The pain was still fresh, and now that I found someone who I was comfortable with, I thought it best to continue seeing her for the time being.

The next week came and went, I cried more, but it was a good cry. She hadn't talked to her friend yet to find out what household product could cause this type of trouble. However, the next time I spoke with her, she gave me a little more of the understanding that I needed as to my "WHY God?"

I told her that I was having trouble with bad thoughts. The anxiety and the recurring dreams of what happened played over and over in my head. They were on constant repeat, and her reply was,

"You are going to have these thoughts for the rest of your life, but in time you will learn to manage them better. Look at the good memories that you remember. Over time, it will be the same for the bad ones, but know that each thought you choose to reflect on is a memory that you can either not think on, or you can allow to consume you."

"You can suffer the pain of change, or suffer remaining the way you are." Joyce Meyers writes in *Battlefield of the Mind*.

As much as she was right, and as much as I needed to hear what she was telling me, I just wanted to turn off my brain for a little while so I could sort it all out, but I knew my mind didn't work that way.

Because of my trauma, my brain was now wired differently. It seemed as if I could no longer think clearly. All thoughts had been diverted to one particular day over and over again. Whether I wanted to think about it or not, I did. Whether I wanted to feel the pain or not, I did.

It would have been much simpler and easier if I had forgotten it all, I told myself. These thoughts that I regularly sifted and rolled over and over kept coming back to me, but in the end, I knew that I wasn't supposed to forget them. They were the fuel to my fire to help me finally move forward. I began to use them to continue the process of healing that I so desperately needed. The more questions I asked, the more I had to go to God and His Word to get the understanding that I needed. Each "why?" I asked was another brick laid to a road that I kept telling myself I never wanted to travel down. Each moment I spent crying was the cleansing that had to happen to wash away the stains of my righteous indignation. I was humbled, and I took the road back to God.

The last and final week I went back to see Dr. Rodriguez, she asked me a question. It came entirely out of left field.

"Now what did you learn from this?"

I wasn't sure she said what I thought she said. "Pardon me?" I say.

"What did you learn from all this?" she asks once more.

It felt as if someone grabbed hold of my neck and was choking me. The room suddenly got hot, and I couldn't hear anything Dr. Rodriguez was saying. I could see her lips moving, but I couldn't understand a word she was saying. Nothing she said made sense.

"What?" I asked, "What have I learned? Are you serious?" Standing to my feet, I knew she could see that I was angry. "Calm down, I didn't mean it that way," she explains.

"What way could you possibly mean it? What could anyone possibly learn from being raped?"

She tries to explain herself, but we were running out of time, and she said she wanted to clarify it the following week. I firmly explain to her that I won't be coming back next week. She knew that the question she just asked was not appropriate at the time and she could see that I was notably upset. I intended to find a Christian counselor to help me filter my thoughts, to clarify what was happening, and to help me transition to a better place than where I currently was, but that one question angered me so much that I canceled any future sessions. She stands, and I reach out to shake her hand so that I can leave. We shake hands, and she says, "I hope you're not too angry with me, I didn't mean it the way you are taking it." In my mind, it no longer mattered. We shake hands, and I walk out the door.

I shake my head, shrug my shoulders and say, "Ok God, it's just going to be you and I," I'm going to need you to help me through this. Saddened by her question, I began to think that she was blaming me. How could she? Out of all the crimes in the world, you can be a victim of them all except for rape. Society tells you it's your fault. You wore the wrong type of clothing, you walked down the wrong street, you talked to the wrong person, and maybe you were not aware of your surroundings. Shame on you for getting yourself in trouble.

This was the time in my walk with God that I finally had to say that it no longer mattered. I had come to the place where it was just God and I, and nothing in between. It no longer mattered how society looked at me, how his family looked at me, and even how I viewed myself at the time. It had been an uphill battle up until this very moment, and I knew that something had to be done. It was time to change my view. The window I had been looking through was very cloudy. It had been stained with the deception of depression, guilt, shame, hurt, fear, and defeat; I couldn't see, it was so foggy, and it was time to wipe it clean. I had to decide on refocusing my thoughts to help myself heal. It didn't matter how many times I had read it in a book or heard Chris's voice telling me that I could do it. It was entirely up to me. No one else could help me. As soon as I had decided to refocus my mind and change my thoughts and ask God to go the distance with me, I knew that it was going to be tough. The battle I had chosen to fight had a massive hold on me, and I was weakened by the many blows that I had sustained by the enemy. Before, it was as if I thought I could do it all by myself, and even though I truly didn't want to, knowing that I was not asking God to help implied that I could do it on my own.

Since I had stopped talking to God and decided to go it alone, the enemy was able to isolate me and beat me down with lies and what ifs. He beat me down because I wasn't prepared. Had I known the Word, I would have been able to cope a little better. My skills would have helped me effectively deal with life even though Craig dealt a blow, the policeman dealt a blow, the doctor dealt a blow and the psychologist dealt a blow. I had to finally ask God to help me. I knew I couldn't do it on my own anymore; it was too much. My world was crashing down around me, and I finally had to let it all go. I had to let go of the hurt Craig dished out, and I had to let go of Sinister and Ivy. If I wanted to live a more productive life, I had to let them all go; not forget anything that happened, but let them go.

Lord...Show Me, My Enemy
Show me, me

Shortly after wanting to be free of the hurt and the feelings that had me going in circles, I found myself wavering on the details that would help me move closer toward forgiveness. I began to think, as the thoughts kept circling like vultures. Had I been on a road that I shouldn't have been on? Was I on that road to self-destruction? Again I ask God some more questions. After sitting in the counselor's office for that short amount of time, I had come to myself and decided to ask God the hard question.

Driving home from the office on that last day, I search my thoughts as each question that I ask pains me. I knew I wasn't prepared for the answers, but I needed the answers. "God, can you show me my enemies?" I asked. "Please show me who is for me and who is against me so I can heal." I put my head in my hands while I sit waiting for the red light to change. I can feel the tears coming, but I do my best to keep them in place. "Suck it up, right now," I tell myself. I look around as I sit at the corner of Dolsten and Shutt Rd. They have just completed the construction on the new Quick Check, and it should be opening soon. I pray again that God would hear my prayers. While I had spoken to Dr. Rodriguez, it felt good talking with someone. I had been holding the pain and frustration in, and it weighed me down. I knew I couldn't take it anymore. I had finally given myself permission to heal. The fear kept me quiet for so long, as well as the stress of wanting to remain normal. I knew I would never be the same again.

During one of my three sessions, I had also learned some of the people I had attached myself to were never going to facilitate any type of healing. I had been down and out for so long that the world was just moving and it felt as if I was standing still, trapped by a memory that seemed like it was always chasing me down. The faster I'd run, the quicker it would come, and I was always tripped up. My shoes were never on tight, my laces were loose, and I couldn't get my knees up high enough to facilitate a longer stride. I ran from this problem, but it walked me down. Crying out to God to open my eyes was all I knew how to do. That's what we are supposed to do. Grandma used to say, *when you don't know what else to do, cry out to God and He will help you.* The Bible says,

"God is our refuge and strength, a very present help in trouble." Psalm 46:1

Knowing all of this, I was still afraid.

Fear

Fear was one of the first things that He showed me. It wasn't just the fear of living, not living, the safety of my children, or even that this terrible thing could happen again. My fears stretched beyond that. I was fearful that God wouldn't be God. I was scared that everything I had learned was a lie. Stumbling right into where the enemy, my real enemy the devil wanted me to be— out of a relationship with God. As I said earlier in a previous chapter, I didn't want to be in a relationship with God anymore. When Kurt Carr sang in his song, "the devil really had me", that was exactly it. I wanted nothing to do with God because of my fear. Not being able to catch this man because

I had no proof of all that he had done to me, and watching him move on with his life caused me great distress. He was not physically in my face all the time, but I imagined that he was "living his best life" and not feeling an ounce of remorse for what he had done to me, and now God was and is the only rectifier of this situation.

"Nothing in all creation is hidden from God's sight. Everything is uncovered and laid bare before the eyes of him to whom we must give account" Hebrews 4:13.

It says in His Word that He is the only one who can make this right, and I was fearful that it wouldn't come to pass. My fear and anxiety caused me to second-guess it all; the love of God, the care that He had for me, the simple fact that He didn't leave me, and His protection. If I couldn't see any of these things, then to me they didn't exist. When God saved my child, I was able to see His love, His protection, His care for me and His protection of my heart because He knew something like that would kill me. At least this is what I believed. I also thought that the rape would have killed me as well; that's why I hid it in my heart under lock and key. It was God who knew how afraid I was, and soon the fear caused me to look at God differently. Fear had me taking a second look at God, checking to see if God was going to be God for me. Once I had my heart locked in on what God could do for me, I expected it to happen because God is God and He wants what's best for us, right? I had forgotten, of course, that God doesn't work for me. I wanted Him to work this thing out for me. It never occurred to me that without any of these things - if God never does any of these things - God is still God. One of the hardest lessons that I had to learn was that God doesn't work for me! God is not my genie and He doesn't owe me a single thing. My fear of the situation caused me to forget what God had already done for me and shifted me in a direction that I ultimately never wanted to go. I had walked away from God simply out of fear. The fear that God wouldn't be a just God and He would allow this man to continue with his life because his actions were justified. The resentment of this train of thought caused even more anger than you could imagine, which brings me to my next enemy. I was angry with God because I refused to see my actions. I refused to look inside myself. I am not justifying his actions by accepting my own, because no one deserves to be raped or drugged for any reason. What I mean is that there are a number of actions that are my own that cause me to be angry at God, and none of them are acceptable.

Anger

After thinking and thinking and thinking some more that God let this happen to me, I was angry. The major reason being that I was under the impression that if I accepted God as my Savior, I was protected and I was covered. Many new believers think the same, as well as non-believers, but it's simply not true. It doesn't necessarily work that way. God does protect us and keep us safe, but being in His will warrants many attacks that the enemy prepares and calculates because we are children of God. This world is wicked and full of corrupt people, and I almost slipped.

The Word says, "Be angry and do not sin." Being angry is not the sin; the sin was rehearsing the act over and over in my mind in anticipation of doing something...sin. I was so mad that I knew how and what I was going to do. It was time to perpetuate the cycle, and keep the hurt going so that I would feel better even if it was for a little while. I felt like I needed it.

Like a drug had been pumped in my veins, I needed to do something to get me back to a state where I felt ok. The anger was controlling me, and if my feelings said go right, I was going right. The enemy began to fan the flames of my rage and used the fact that I was hurting to keep my attention. I had blamed God for it all, and my anger kept me blind to my own actions. How did I play a part in the breakdown of my relationship? Could all of this have been avoided if I had left when things initially went bad? How about the fact that I didn't even give God the opportunity to heal Craig. I'm not saying stay in an abusive relationship, I'm saying, leave and help him or her get some counselling possibly. Ultimately, there were other avenues to take, and I explored none of them with God. I wanted things to change instantly, and I now know that things could have never been fixed that way.

At the reception of our wedding, our guests expressed to us the need to keep God first in our lives. Pray and ask God for the things that we needed, and also wait on Him—charged with these instructions I had great hope in us, in our marriage, and in the man I married. However, we were spiritually deficient in all areas and lacked a relationship with God, and honestly I had no understanding that we needed it as bad as we did. It was not until we had crossed this very road that I had finally come to discern the need for a relationship with God, and arrested by my anger, perplexed by a direction that would carry me back to the 'me' of yesterday, I couldn't and didn't want to let it go. The pain was crippling, and my focus was no longer on a relationship. I had no care for anything, and it was all I could see, feel, taste, hear, and I just lived in it. Pain was my third enemy, and it caused me not to see God as God. It was as if I was going crazy. The hurt wouldn't stop.

Pain

God allowed me to see the pain. Its constant ache charted a course in waters that were unknown to me. I ran because it was all I knew how to do, and it was all I wanted to do. I didn't want to help Craig because I felt he should have known that this would have caused such a divide in us, and I couldn't forgive him for putting my son's head through the wall. It was the pain that I had to get away from, and yet no matter how far I ran, I still found myself brought full circle of the very same pain that I was trying to avoid. The pain of being drugged and raped might not seem so bad to some because you don't remember all the details, but the thought of someone coming into my safe place and violating me while I slept has caused some damage that no one can erase. A movie of the details that I do remember plays constantly in my head, and most days I don't even want to sleep. I think about what happened all the time, and learned that certain images trigger these thoughts, like opening a wine bottle or just sipping on a glass of wine. I'm more aware of my surroundings now than ever before, and I always think that something will go wrong at any moment. Lastly, I no longer feel safe, anywhere. The pain of this has caused so much damage that I had to try my best to get a hold of it before it overtook me any longer. This pain had me thinking about how I was going to get revenge, and even though I knew it was wrong, I kept telling myself I needed it. It had to stop; all I wanted was for the pain to stop. The ache that you could never see, and the thoughts that crept up on me without a moment's notice. This pain gave me a new outlook on God and life, and now the real enemy was pleased.

As hard as it was, not one single day has gone by that I don't think about what has happened to me. I still feel like I have to dissect every moment. It was my second job, and despite the exhaustion in my mind, I worked it. From the moment I opened my eyes, my mind went to work on the facts. I punched the clock from the time my eyes opened until the time my eyes closed. This mental agony invaded every inch of my brain. Weariness seized my body, attacked my mind, and overwhelmed my spirit, causing an unbearable longing for rest. Not the type of rest you get when you go to sleep and wake in the morning, no not like that. I craved the milk like the late Michael Jackson had. It would have been just fine if I had fallen asleep and not woken up for a couple of years. Anything to escape the pain that had seduced me and had become my new best friend. The pain that I wanted to avoid was his middle name. Pain was the car I drove to work. Pain was the food I ate. Pain was the house I cleaned. The pain was my everything, and I couldn't get rid of it. I couldn't shake it; I couldn't let it go. I didn't know how, and I didn't know what to do. Then I realized that most people don't know how, or what to do either. Some people don't know how to move forward. I didn't know how to move forward, and I didn't know how to "GET OVER IT"! The obscenity of those three words makes my skin crawl. You can never tell a person to get over something that you have never gone through. The funny thing is that this is what you hear from people all the time who have never gone through something. When I say SOMETHING, I mean the kind of SOMETHING that makes you question your existence, which is precisely where I was. I was standing between the type of SOMETHING that made me question GOD, and what I already knew. That SOMETHING for me would have been my current offense of rape. For you, it can be ANYTHING. It could be the death of a child, the senseless act of violence, or any of the same things that we go through on a daily basis. Usually, when people go through similar trauma, they have compassion and empathy for each other. They have a simple understanding.

I know it's not easy. I know how it feels when all strength is gone and your will to live has been ripped from underneath you like a rug. When days turn into nights and you don't even realize it. I walked and walked through my days as if I were in some dark hole. Round and round in a circle I went, talking to myself, telling myself what had happened almost as if it were some creepy out-of-body experience. Only I was not hovering over my body watching what was going on. I was watching myself try to figure it all out. THEN IT HIT ME LIKE A TON OF BRICKS....CINDER BLOCKS.

Truth is I was raped, but now I was giving power to this man, and I began to rape myself.

Each thought that I kept reliving, I was raping myself. Every moment that I wanted to relive for answers and clues as to the exact detail that plagued my soul was also the same detail that caused my heart to ache. The who of the matter, the what of the matter, the when, the why, and the how sent aftershocks through me as if the earthquake that stole my joy was not enough devastation. The earthquake of rape wasn't enough, and I still wanted revenge.

Chapter 10

Lord I Want Revenge

Then said he unto the disciples, "It is impossible but that offenses will come but woe unto him, through whom they come!" Luke 17:1 KJV

Jesus said to his disciples: "Things that cause people to stumble are bound to come, but woe to anyone through whom they come." Luke 17:1 NIV

The pain in my heart blinded my ability to comprehend this passage completely. In the Word, it says that offenses will come, and it is impossible for them not to come. Accosted by this offense, I had to ask God what to do. I wanted revenge so bad I had to ask God, "How do you turn the cheek when no justice has been served? How do you turn the cheek when the perpetrator has a new life and is able to walk around freely, knowing that they got away with everything they have done?" I just wanted to dish out the same portion of hurt. I wanted to do it, and I explained to God that I wanted it to be me. "Let me do it, Lord," I asked. Amidst my tears, with a broken heart, again I felt I knew what was best. From the moment that I put all the pieces together, I had begun to form a plan. If they only knew what I was thinking, I promise you they would not have smiled in my face like everything was ok. My thoughts were not my own.

"Be angry and do not sin," Ephesians 4:26

I heard it clear as day. I told myself it didn't matter if I hurt anyone else because I was hurting. I had somehow been able to keep this boiling pot of feelings from spilling over, but this time I was unable to. I looked at the entire situation of what happened, and my heart hardened. Like Pharaoh, it was all about me. This time something was different. In my mind I was convinced by the enemy that it would be acceptable to do what they did - take from them the same amount of peace that they stole from me. By any means necessary I was going to deal the same blow, make them feel the pain that I felt.

After the initial conversation with Sinister and another talk with Ivy, I had planned their expected end. The place that I had elected to stock up on the hurt and pain I found myself drowning in was the place that kept my focus. I felt played. Sinister chose me because he had made a bet with his friends that he would be able to seduce me. Not just me, but both Ivy and me. Now, Ivy knew what was what and decided to roll with it, but then she caught feelings. Later, to cover it all up, she came to me with the sob story and acted like she didn't know anything. It was Sinister's plan all along to do exactly what he did. What did he gain? That was something I was not privy to, but I was the one who ultimately lost. It was just a game. I was just a game, and I got played, and after this information came to me, it would have been well with my soul if God had turned them all over to me. However, that was never going to be the case. God is the Author and Finisher of our faith. He is the one who will avenge the hurt and the wronged according to His will, not mine. I had learned this; except, I wanted to be the avenger.

Dearly beloved, avenge not yourselves, but rather give place unto wrath: for it is written, Vengeance is mine; I will repay, saith the Lord. Romans 12:19

I wanted to pluck those words from the Bible and forget that I had read them, but all too many times that's what we want to do. We pick and choose what we think is best to suit our life and we throw out the rest. In spite of what I knew, I would have been wrong if I had finally done what I wanted to do. In my weakest, which was at that exact moment, I believed that taking revenge on them would make me feel better, even if it was just for a little while. That moment of release was all I wanted, and I was on the verge of taking it, and then I simply remembered: "Vengeance is the Lord's." I'm more than sure God brought this back to my remembrance. God has a way of doing just that.

But the Advocate, the Holy Spirit, whom the Father will send in my name, will teach you all things and will remind you of everything I have said to you. John 14:26

Even still, I wanted to do something.

Vengeance is Mine

If I could watch Craig go through the same thing, I would be satisfied; that's what I told myself.

If I could see him get run over by a truck, there would be a sense of satisfaction in me that knows he has gotten what he deserves. But, death is too good for him. I honestly thought to myself, *do you believe it will make all the hurt go away?* For a small fraction of a second, I did. I thought that was indeed what I needed to heal. I needed to delve out the punishment. I was to be the one to deal the final blow which, in turn, brings him to his knees and helps him to see how his actions plagued me for years. Somehow I felt justified. That's what I kept telling myself. For a short time, I said to myself that this was what I needed. The thoughts crept into my mind of how to bring him to his knees, and also how to dish out the same if not the worst amount of pain that he put me through. It was my right, right? An eye for an eye, right? Whether he knew that this was my worst fear or not, I felt compelled to dish out the same amount of hurt that he so dishonorably dished out onto me.

    Not thinking about a single thing except my pain, I began to think about the different ways that I could really hurt Craig. The days seemed endless about how I could hurt all of them. Days went by, plan after plan, I had come up with some evil things. Some so evil I knew they could not have come from me. Whispers of what could shake his foundation, just like he did mine came to the surface. I had taken the devil's hand, and he was leading me to a place I had never been.

"This will bring him to his knees, just like he did to you."

"If that's not good enough, you can also try this...maybe even do something like this."

The thoughts would come one right after another; many, many ideas came. So much so that I began to let the enemy take me closer and closer to that ledge again. Now, he wanted me to destroy myself, and what better way to get me to forfeit what God had for me. The enemy expressed the need for me shut my mouth, and soon he led me to constantly do things that would keep me from God and what He has for me. I knew that it wasn't GOD talking to me. "God's voice has no sin in it," said Steve Harvey on his morning show. No, I knew who it was, but I began to entertain the thoughts because I was hurt and even still I was not able to forgive.

I didn't want to forgive. I wanted revenge, and not just any kind of revenge, the kind that comes from my two hands. I wanted to be the one to dish out the pain. With my hands, I wanted to hurt him just as much as I had been hurt. Let me forget the beginning and skip to the end, come up with a conclusion and play the victim so that I too can irrationally come to some justification as to the why, and dish out the consequence of his actions like he did. I wanted to be just like him; wicked and prospering. To be like Sinister and his friends, it was all a joke. To be like Ivy, because it is what it is, *you like it, I love it* echoed.

"But what about your sin?" God said. "What about all that YOU have done?"

Inclined to answer His question with another question, I just thought for a moment. God and I parlay, and I hear: "Again this is what it means in the Bible when it calls for forgiveness! If you already know that I said vengeance is mine, and I will repay them for what they did, then it is your job to let them go." My thoughts were, "BUT, Lord I don't want to forgive any of them. I want revenge, and I want to watch. Let me be a fly on the wall." I firmly held onto the pain of yesterday, afraid to give it to God. One hand on the pain and the other on a gun to help me help them meet their maker. God taps me on the shoulder once again:

"Are you sinless? Is there any sin greater than another?" I shuffle for words, but He continues:

"Did you make the heavens or the earth? Are you God? Why do to them what they did to you? How do you know that will even work? Just because something hurts you doesn't necessarily mean it will hurt them. They may recover quicker, and then what? Should you keep going with your cycle of revenge until you feel better? Leave them to me. Vengeance is mine." Romans 12:19 God finally placed it on my heart that it was not my job to punish any of them, especially not Craig. If it was in His will, then it will be done.

Cast All Your Cares

There was nothing left for me to do, but just that. Leave it all up to God even though I sincerely didn't want to. I wanted to show them that you can't do this to people and get away with it. I wanted to be the only reason that they turned from their wicked ways and never do something like this to anyone ever again; but that was not what I was supposed to do. Craig could have presumably had the same thoughts. It finally occurred to me that I had to forgive them. Not because they deserved it, but because I had been held captive for way too long and each day seemed longer than the next. The consequences of my actions as well as theirs had brought me to this junction, and for me I could quickly go left, not forgive and help them see God in all His glory and splendor, or forgive them all sincerely and give them over to God to do as He pleases; whether it be to punish them or not, God truly knew their hearts. If He chooses to punish them let it be so, and if He decides not to, then let that be so as well. The time had come where I had to cast all my cares on Him. 1 Peter 5:7. The one who created me. The one who saved my son. The God of Abraham, Isaac, and Jacob.

    I had to finally let it all go before the pain and stress of it all killed me. It was time to let God be God in my life. The time that I wasted being angry, upset, drained, and hurt went on for far too long. It was time to get my emotions and feelings in check; they had ruled my thinking for almost three years, and I almost lost my life because of it. I had been on a journey to dig two graves - actually three - but I was so angry and focused on the hurt for such a long time that my thoughts were not my own any longer.

    As I stated (in an earlier chapter) whatever ideas came to my mind, I chose to think on, and that was a perilous place to be. Ushered back to the ledge and ready to jump simply because the thoughts popped into my mind. I never factored in these destructive thoughts as each weighed me down. They were not my own. I elected to feed off these feelings so I could facilitate the same amount of hurt. I knew I would have been wrong, and no sooner than that God helped me. I felt another enormous weight lifted off me, and I could finally breathe again, even if it were for a little while.

Forgiveness

Could Craig go to God and say to Him, "Lord I had to rape her because she was cheating on me"? I wasn't cheating on him, but that's neither here nor there. He never realized that the only reason I knew something was wrong with me was because I was faithful to him. I felt the pain of everything. After waking up, I knew something was wrong, but I was not able to put all the pieces together until it was all said and done. The enemy had him sold on the lies that I was still cheating on him. Could he go to God and say that he was justified in doing what he did because I did what I did? Could I go to God and say, "God I deserve to dish out this revenge because of what he did to me"? Certainly not. His actions will never be justified, nor can I beg God to let mine be justified to take his life.

Do not repay anyone evil for evil. Be careful to do what is right in the eyes of everyone. If possible, as far as it depends on you, live at peace with everyone. Do not take revenge, my dear friends, but leave room for God's wrath, for it is written: It is mine to avenge; I will repay, says the Lord…Do not be overcome by evil, but overcome evil with good. Romans 12:14

Further instruction is given on how to treat your enemies in which He states:

If your enemy is hungry, feed him; if he is thirsty, give him something to drink. In doing this, you will heap burning coals on his head.

I wish with everything in me that I can say that I have graduated to this here Scripture, but I honestly have not. I wanted to forgive them all, but I didn't know how. I elected to remove myself from their presence as much as possible, and keep my distance for fear that the devil would finally convince me that it was ok to do what I originally wanted to do. I was running from evil. Psalm 37-29.

Had I not walked away; I knew we would have all been in trouble.

Certainly, forgiveness was long overdue. It had taken me more years than I wanted to admit to understand that it was more important to forgive than to harbor the feelings of hatred any longer. If I had not asked God to show me my enemies, God would not have also shown me, me. I could have been my worst enemy had I gone through with any of the evil thoughts. No, I forgave them, because I had to, and I forgave them because it was stealing my life from me. It was taking my joy and robbing me of my purpose. I could not allow the enemy another second of my time, whether it be from crying, being angry, hurting inside, depressed, ashamed, or scared. No longer would I bathe in the loss and failure of my infirmities. I finally forgave them; but it wasn't easy, and it wasn't overnight.

Not only did I have to forgive them, but I also had to forgive myself. There was a mound of guilt that I had to dig myself out from under, and shame also had me looking over my shoulder, wondering who felt that I deserved exactly what I got. A still small voice whispered to me and fostered the beginning of my new outlook on life:

"Let he who is without sin among you, cast the first stone" John 8:7

I had sinned, and it was my sin that led me to their forgiveness. It was painstakingly hard to reach this level of spiritual awareness. There was a part of me that wanted to avenge the little girl in me that had been violated. However, how could I then go to God and ask Him for forgiveness for any of my sins—past, present, or future? It would not be so easy for me to forget that I too needed forgiveness. I had not been all the way right in this turpitude, but I was not all the way wrong. Some may disagree with me, but we are all entitled to our opinion. Chastened by God to the point of my new moral enlightenment, I had begun to see the value of John 8:7 in my life. I had sinned and needed forgiveness, whether this time or the next, and so had they. Be that as it may, God knew my heart, He knew what I needed, and I had finally decided to let them go. I could no longer harbor an ounce of anger any longer. It was time to forgive them and give them to God.

Chapter 11

Lord I Know You Love Me

All my life I had to fight…that's a line from my favorite movie, "The Color Purple." Oprah Winfrey's character referred Celie because she had advised Harpo to beat on; to get her to act right…now I had to fight. I had to fight this battle back to God. I had to educate myself on who God was in my life, and it was apparent that I had absolutely no idea who He was. I thought I knew Him, but now I had to really get to know Him. As I began to look back, I knew my hurt and my selfish behavior would not allow me see that God did care about me. I was consumed by every thought, every second of pain, and every tear that dropped from my eyes. It was all about me. It was all about what I needed from God. Never had I ever gone through something like this, and because I was so consumed with my feelings and how I hurt, I could not hear from God anymore or even want Him to speak to me. It would have been much easier to try to forget. I wanted the easy. The simple life, the secure, and the sure things were what I longed for, but this walk with God was never going to be easy.

I thought that if I gave my life over to Christ, I would be blessed into a new world of protection - that nothing could harm me. I thought that by giving my life over to God, He would cover me for the rest of my days. After further research, I had come to understand that many, many new Christians believe the same as I had. The Bible tells us that our days with God, or without God, are few and full of trouble. Job 14:1. It was time to change me, my thoughts and my ways. Should I stay and continue to let the enemy push my buttons? Should I stay in a state of confusion, hurt and fear for the rest of my life? Tripping over these questions, I wanted to have the answers, but I had no idea what to do. This life experience I was living was only to get by. It was not to make it to the next day nor the next month, I was merely trying to make it to the next second. Since time had begun to stand still, I didn't even want to think that far ahead. No! I had to take back what the enemy stole, as they say in church. I couldn't allow my adversary to have this much hold over me any longer.

The enemy had me convinced that God didn't love me. Me, the one who He created in His own image (Genesis 1:27). Me, the one that He knew before I was conceived (Jeremiah 1:4-5). Me, the one He had chosen when He planned to create this world (Ephesians 1:11-12). Me! The one who is not a mistake (Psalm 139:15-16). Me! The one who is fearfully and wonderfully made (Psalm 139:14).

I had been listening to the enemy tell me lies, intently. The father of lies fed me each morning, noon and night because my grief allowed him to enter my life and cause such uncertainty. I ate it up - every drop, as if I had not already been fed with the truth. I listened to this four-course meal before me and ate up the shame of being raped, whether it was my fault or not. The words bitter, sour, contrite, and rash. Yet, without missing a beat, I listened to the new story. It was as if I had sat and let the enemy tell me all these crazy things about my best friend. ME! These storms had been raging inside me for too long. I had to silence the doubt and get back to the basics.

It had finally come a time for me to address my demons, and speak to my storms.

Peace Be Still

One by one I had to deal with each storm; Storm Craig, Storm Sinister, and Storm Ivy, as well as my misconception of God. I had to deal with them one on one because trying to group everything together made things even more confusing and it drained me. Dropping the psychologist like she was hot didn't help me either because I had no outlet anymore, and the hospital visit along with the police officer helped me find a place within myself that absolutely no one knew about. I internalized it all.

Craig had proceeded to tell everyone that I was crazy. He even went as far as calling some of my friends to try and tell them that he wanted to help me, but I wouldn't let him. One by one Craig called to try and hide what he had done to me and to discredit me. He was trying to clean up the mess that he created by making me look insane. As much as it hurt to know that he was doing this, it didn't bother me. I knew what happened and that was what mattered the most to me. The hardest part of this particular storm was the fact that I finally had to talk about what happened. I had to face this fear of my family treating me just like the police officer or the doctor in the emergency room did. In my mind, I thought I would be left alone in all of this. I thought there would be no shoulder to cry on, or anyone to tell me to think positively. I would be left alone drowning in my thoughts like before. Listening to the enemy torment me while he ushers me to the ledge to entice me to jump once again. I was scared to speak about it, but whatever the outcome and whether I was prepared or not, it was finally time.

One of the first people besides my husband who I poured my heart out to was my sister. She was my sister-in-Christ. We were not blood-related (more like sisters from another mister) but I loved her, and I knew she loved me. We met in church. I asked her if we could talk because I could no longer hold the pain in. We agreed to meet at a local diner off of Western Avenue, in the heart of Albany.

It was a cute little place, hidden by the hustle and bustle of a strip mall, seeing that I hadn't even noticed it was there until Michelle suggested the place to meet. She reminded me so much of Rae Dawn Chong. Her curls always popped and I secretly envied her for them. I'd give up this 4C hair for her beautiful bouncy curls any day. She was bright light like the sun and always had a positive thing to say, not to mention a fantastic ability to see things from a positive perspective most days.

As I walk up to the door, I can see her sitting inside. The huge glass window exposed all the charm of the insides. Warm colors decorate the walls, and earth tones blend with each chair. It was as if I was going to take a seat in my living room. The backs of some of the booths looked as if the fabric chosen could have come from a movie set. She is sitting in the middle of the restaurant adorned with chairs all around her, waiting for me. I was a little late; quite possibly because deep down the fear of her rejection was going to be more than I could handle. Life seemed to stand still at that moment as I tried my best to fight back the tears, but she gives me this look, and I couldn't hold them back any longer. She sat intently listening as I poured my heart out to her. She didn't say much, just sat and listened to me. The first question that came from her lips was, "Why didn't you say something before?"

"I was terrified to tell anyone what happened." The water began to flow, and I felt a rush of relief like I had never felt before. I had finally gotten the courage to begin talking about what had happened, and as hard as it was to speak the words, "I WAS RAPED" into the world, they were equally hard to accept. I sat shaking, but I had to continue. I vomited to her the details that I remembered because I was afraid if I stopped I wouldn't have the courage to continue. We sat in silence for a moment, and we both cried a little. "If I could forget that the day I was raped had ever occurred and wipe it clean from my memory, I assume I would be better for it, except I was wrong." She sat and listened. "Deep down inside I believed I would die if something like this ever happened to me. That was the reason to keep this thought in solitary confinement, locked away from all. It frightened me so bad that I needed to keep this to myself rather than give anyone the ammunition to hurt me."

"BUT GOD"

It felt good to finally let her in. For a short moment, she was the world, and she didn't reject me. She didn't know it though. Had she treated me in the least like the doctor or the cop, I probably would have sunk further into depression and no one would have been able to reach me.

After we finished talking, we prayed. This time it felt different. It seemed as if I could feel God's presence once more. It took me back to when God had revealed himself to me moments before I had almost run over Gabriel. I knew deep down that God hadn't left me, but during this time it felt as if

God had stopped by to hear our prayers. Soon after we said our goodbyes, I began my drive home, and thoughts of Craig and his actions were on my mind. "He has no idea," I tell myself. Craig had no idea what he had done. His efforts proved to me that I didn't die, and I am stronger now than I have ever been in my entire life. He awakened the sleeping giant in me that I didn't even know I had. I am no longer afraid of anything. For that, I must tell him THANK YOU.

This storm was an open door to a new beginning with God. This storm helped me to see God for who God is. My Deliverer, my Healer, my Refuge, my Strength, my Guide, my Helper, my Provider. God is my all in all, and this storm finally helped me to see My God for who He is, and not who I thought He was.

Sinister

Before Sinister and I had even so much as kissed, I had considered him a good friend. We shared a love for food, and it was fun trying new things with him. We often watched the food network, talked about the thought of eating in the restaurants that piqued our interest and then set out to visit in the future. Obviously, something that I should have been doing with my husband, but Craig was extremely old school. He had a love for food as well, but trying new things was not his thing. He didn't want anything except soul food. Nothing else, ever. I don't blame Craig for not sharing my passion for food, but it would have been nice to be able to share that with him. Maybe I didn't give him enough time, or even a chance, but I knew I couldn't go back. As I took a closer look at Sinister and our situationship, I realized he and I should have never been. He had given me too many opportunities to doubt us. He was very outgoing; he could speak to anyone and seemed happy most of the time. Some days he was a little more reserved than others, but he loved to laugh and have fun. With his extroverted personality, he took command of a room as soon as he walked in. Whether he knew anyone or not, he worked it like it was magic. There were also days where he spent time with his ex-girlfriends; they would usually go and have breakfast some mornings. One afternoon, in particular, he said that a friend of his needed his help to replace a telephone jack in her home. Sinister even bought one of them a dog, of which I wasn't too happy with him for at the time. He was definitely on a different path than I, and I should have said my goodbyes a long, long time ago, but shame on me for having a little bit of hope that things could change. I most certainly think this is where I had gone wrong, and I can't blame him for a single thing that I helped him get away with. I had to also look at what I allowed him do.

During the time that I was going through and understanding what had happened to me, part of me spent so much time wondering if things could have been different. Unfortunately, I already knew the truth. I had to search my memory to times when Sinister and I began. How did things go? Was I happy? Was he happy? Was he with someone else then? Could he possibly do this again? Would he do it again? The last question struck a nerve because I already knew what the answer was. In the beginning, our friendship helped me see him, except I chose to overlook who he was because Craig and I were not vibing. I decided to ignore his actions even though he told me who he was. Before things escalated between Sinister and I, it was important to me that I went to him to explain how I was feeling. I didn't want to feel a certain way, and he wasn't feeling the same. It would have been easy to put my feelings to bed had he said, "No that isn't what we are doing." Instead, he said, "I feel the same way, and I'd never hurt you." No matter what he let come out of his mouth, it was more important to look at his actions than listen to what he said. Looking back, I knew exactly when I let my guard down and exactly where I went wrong. He was always going to be with Ivy, and that was why he talked about her in such a bad way, because he was always interested in her. He wanted to win, at the expense of nothing more than someone's feelings—my feelings. You know the saying: hurt people hurt people, and we were both searching for something. Obviously not the same things, but we ultimately found it in the end. I can forgive him because we both made choices. I'm not even mad at him. I just never thought he would be able to do something like this. I mean we were all friends for years. We would see each other every single day for about seven years. I likened us to be some sort of work family. These were the people who helped me get back home to my family safely. He prided himself on his integrity and talked about everyone else who didn't have any, but the more I listened, and I mean really listened to his words, I wanted to kick myself for falling in love with his potential and not who he was. Even though we did everything together, it seemed like none of it mattered to him. He just wanted his cake and to be able to eat it too. When I asked him why he chose Ivy, he replied, "I never thought you were going to find out." My mother's voice echoes in my mind, "What's done in the dark." The questions of *would*

I, or could I have been happy, would he ever do it again, was he already doing it, had already been answered.

Now, had you asked me these questions a couple of years ago I would have been furious, bitter even, but I am better for it. We were never meant to be anything more than friends. I have to THANK HIM for his choices, and for finally allowing me to see the truth, which in turn facilitated better options on my part whether I would like to continue to deal with his behavior. We all make decisions, some we regret and some we learn from. I am so grateful to God that I had made a better choice this time. I am not saying this man is a bad person; he just wasn't the right person for me. His love for me would have never let him even consider Ivy. It's not bad that he wasn't for me, it's not even bad that he was who he was or he did what he did, because in the end, life is about making decisions. Life is about the choices you make, and who am I to judge him for the choices that he has made or is making. I had made plenty of bad decisions myself. In the end, if we don't learn from our bad choices, we can expect a remedial class and another trip around the same mountain. This time, I had to conquer this mountain because I was determined never to go back to this same area in my life. This storm put me on my knees crying out to God and asking Him which direction I should go. This storm had me looking to the hills from whence cometh my help. Psalm 121. This storm had me finally consulting God and asking which way I should go.

Ivy

Even though Ivy and I worked with each other every day for years, I had finally realized that we only did just that. We worked together. We may have also shared tears when her boyfriend died, we might have even laughed at a couple of jokes here and there, even went out and ate a couple of times for our birthdays; but in the end, we were never friends. Our relationship didn't cross paths too much outside of the job. I can't even remember talking on the phone outside of work. We had a working relationship, and that was about it. I must admit I thought it to be more than it was, but when I take a hard look back at what we shared, it was only Sinister. I know why she came to me and told me why she was with him, and it wasn't to say to her best friend or her sister, as she called me, but to tell me that they were together. She just wanted me to know. During our conversation when I initially found out about her and Sinister, she even went as far as telling me that he had been after her for a long time and she finally gave in. I'm not sure why she had to do it that way, but it is what it is. I don't blame her for anything. This just helps me take a closer look at the people I call my friends. It's now much easier to put everyone in a category. T.D. Jakes explained in a sermon. You have three types of friends.

He characterized each friendship by an association of three different types of people in three different ways:

Confidants

Those people who love you unconditionally. Whether right or wrong, up or down, the people who will be in your corner even when you're wrong. They are the ones who will get in trouble with you and for you. These people will never allow anyone talk bad about you. They are the ones who you can share anything with. Friends who are the gatekeepers of all your crazy secrets. They will be there to help you reach your goals, and they will push you to be better and do better.

Constituents

These people are not into you. They are into what you are for. They are only for what you are for. They don't want the same things as you. They want what's convenient. If they meet someone who will help them further their agenda, they will leave you and cling to the next person. They are only with you because of what you can do for them for the moment.

Comrades

These people are not for you. They are against what you are against. These people team up to fight a greater enemy, and when the enemy is defeated, they will leave and desert you.

This storm asked me to reevaluate my circle. I had to take a closer look at the people that I believed God had placed in my life. This storm blessed me with a new outlook on friendship. Whether I had been friends for 25 years with someone, or even two years, it was time to look at the people who had been taking this life journey with me. Had I been feeding them, or were they feeding me?

By feeding me, I mean encouraging me, helping me, and working things out with me. Had our paths crossed for just a moment in time, or was it supposed to be a lifetime? Each person I called a friend was now in my sight. It was tough for me to make friends. As I stated earlier, I never really trusted anyone. It seemed to me that each person had a hidden agenda, and I didn't feel like being used. So most of the time I had people that I'd talk to, but very rarely considered friends. The people that I considered friends were the ones I could help hide a body for. Don't judge me! Those people are the ones I could go to the ends of the earth with, and they didn't even have to ask. Whenever I said, "I got you", that's precisely what it meant - you wouldn't have to worry about a thing.

I had a friend whom I loved dearly. She was what I considered my best friend. I asked her to be my son's godmother. I knew her for a very long time, and it wasn't until I had to travel down this road did I discern she was not traveling with me. It is true when they say, "If you want to know who your real friends are, get into trouble or go through something." In the beginning, when I first started telling my family and friends what happened, it would have never occurred to me that she would be the one to doubt me. I had known her for 22 years, or at least I thought I knew her. She asked a couple of questions, but it was her tone and the way she asked the questions that I knew she didn't believe anything that I was saying. When Sinister and I had become friends, I wanted him to know my best friend as well. I wanted him to get to know her. She was everything to me at the time. I would have categorized her as a confidant very easily. We shared so much together, and we did everything with each other. I talked to her just about every single day. However, it wasn't until I had been raped that she showed she wasn't for me. I read text messages from her to Sinister on his phone, of her telling him that she didn't care what I said or how I felt because she loved him, and she and Sinister were best friends. Could there have been more between the two of them? Who knows, but I had given Sinister way more credit than he was worth. The text hurt, but it was a truth that I needed. That was the nail that sealed our dysfunction. It hurt, but in the end, it was best for us both. If my best friend wasn't for me, I'd rather find out than believe something different. Reading through his text further, there were things I discovered about my best friend that I would never have thought were possible. She laughed at my dysfunction when I was crying for help. "She has PTSD lol," was another text. Of course, some people would say, "Not like this, I wouldn't want to find out like this." However, it wasn't so much as how I found out, but the simple reality is that I found out and it was something I needed to know. I believe the storm with Ivy helped me evaluate my circle. I had to determine who was for me, and quickly determine who wasn't. My circle of friends has gotten much tighter, and I'm forever grateful for Ivy. To her, I must say Thank you. Without going through this life-changing event, I wouldn't have known who was indeed for me, or who was against me. I'd still assume to know the truth, and now I am more careful with whom I share my time with. I have even prayed to God to have a better selection of friends who will help me reach my destiny.

A Simple Misunderstanding

When I was going through all of this dysfunction, it was not easy. Every place I turned, I faced immense pain, confusion, and difficulty in every direction. It was my misconception of God that kept me living in this flawed perspective. Whether I was at home, or whether I was at work, the fire was turned up. I had to look inward at all the trouble I had caused myself and the stress that had piled on me. All of which had me looking at God. I had blamed him, and my initial reaction was why He didn't protect me. Couldn't You have given me a sign, helped me go a different direction or something? I know now that God doesn't work that way. God could have literally been screaming at me to go in a different direction whether it was Sinister, Ivy, or Craig, and I wouldn't have heard Him. I was so set on what I wanted to do, and I initially thought each decision was what was best for me.

If I had prayed before each major decision, I'm more than sure that the outcome would have been different. Had I prayed before marrying Craig whether we had children or not, had I prayed about a relationship with Sinister, or even had I prayed about a friendship with Ivy, some of these troubles could have been avoided. Friendships are just as meaningful as a relationship with God. Each one has the possibility to remove you from God's purpose and the good things that He wants for you and your life. I had not considered this at any time in my life until now. It wasn't that I was someplace that I shouldn't have been; it was a combination of all the trouble I had endured.

Even King Solomon, known as the wisest man who ever lived, not only in the Bible but of the entire world, prayed to God for wisdom:

Give your servant, therefore, an understanding mind to govern your people that I may discern between good and evil, for who is able to govern this great people 1 Kings 3:9

God appeared to Solomon in a dream at night and said, "Ask! What shall I give you?" 1 Kings 3:5. Solomon, knowing that he was still young in mind, had asked God to give him "an understanding of heart to judge your people, that I may discern between good and evil. In further reading of 1 Kings 3, God was pleased with Solomon that he did not ask for long life, wealth, or the death of his enemies. Instead, he asked to discern the hearts of man. God was extremely pleased. God gave him a wise and understanding heart and said, "There will be no one like you." He also gave him what he did not ask for, both riches and honor 1 Kings 3:13. Had I been as wise, to even go to God and pray for discernment so that I could have never been in a situation like this, quite possibly things could have been different. My misconception of who God was in my life, His love for me, and His purpose for my life caused me more trouble than I care to admit. The only good part is that my life isn't over, and I can begin anew right where I am.

Each storm was designed for a particular purpose. Each storm brought about a new meaning to my life; all I had to do was pick up the magnifying glass and take a closer look. Once I changed my perspective and asked God for insight into the truth, He took me by the hand and opened up every crevice of these storms for me. It was a time such as this to be able to see the meaning of God's love. Each storm, as I walk in a new direction with God, so I'd learn to trust him. One storm to recharge my faith, and get to know God for who He is. The second storm to remove me from people who are not for me, and the last storm so I'd recognize the people who   are.

God could have left me in all my moral deficiency, but He loved me too much to let me keep one foot in the world and one foot in the Kingdom. Looking on the surface, I was paralyzed by my initial reaction and left shorted by the hand of God. Not in any way shape or form was and could God's hand be short. It was my reaction to God that shortened His hand and left me paralyzed. Soon I was gifted by His allowance of circumstances that opened up my vision so I could see more clearly.

The harsh reality was a realization of why the storms had been allowed, and inevitably what I needed.

Chapter 12

Revelations

"For there is nothing hidden that will not be disclosed and nothing concealed that will not be known or brought out into the open" Luke 8:17.

Mom always said, "What's done in the dark will always come to light."

Killing myself would have been one of the worst mistakes I could have ever made. Not only because this life was a gift from God, but also because I would have caused so much more pain. Intentionally or unintentionally, the results would still be the same. A family racked with guilt and shame which no doubt had the opportunity to transform into a generational curse. That's how these things begin. A pain that would have no end, and a cycle that would continue if only I would let it. The saying "hurt people hurt people" stays at the front of my mind. My pain will further perpetuate the cycle of pain and inflict more pain on all of my loved ones. Therefore, moving the cycle of pain from my children to my grandchildren and so on and so on. Soon they think it's ok to take their own life because I had shown them the way to the conclusion of hurt. The ultimate answer to the lifelong problem seems to be fixed by simply taking one's life instead of pressing through the pain. Of course, none of this would be easy. Not the taking of one's life nor the pushing through the pain, but the ultimate victory for me was in seeing this through.

    Sitting in the car on the way home from church, before I spoke to my storms, I still had an issue with wanting to give up. The thoughts lingered like a black cloud on a sunny day. It didn't just stop when I got up and got out of the closet. It still came and went. My adversary was after me, and he wouldn't stop. As we were driving home, I was sitting in the passenger seat, and I just began to cry. The tears came and went as usual. And then clear as day I heard God say, "You're going to give him all that money." In my mind, I'm trying to process it quickly. There was no longer any time to get it wrong. Then it came to me. He was talking about my life insurance policy. At first, I got mad, and then I started laughing. He was right! In an attempt to stop the pain yet again I would still allow him to come out on top. He would win. The money would eventually wind up in his hands because he has to take care of the children if something happens to me. Not only had he tried to tell everyone that I was crazy, but I would help his lies become truth. "See, I told you she was crazy. She wound up taking her own life." It wasn't just his words that rang in my mind. It was that he could tell my children anything and I would never be able to tell them the truth. Suddenly, during that ride home, God finally released me from the pain I had felt for so long. I was enlightened, lighter, and stronger all at the same time. Mentally, another door unlocked and the enemy no longer had a hold on me. That was the last time I felt the need to end my life. That was the last time I thought no one loved or needed me. That was the last time God and I had a conversation about me and my pain. I finally began to understand the journey and this process.

I've always known and believed that God has a plan for our lives. It is God's WILL for us that we follow the plan. However, there was a time when I didn't fully understand what that was. Fighting my way back to God, I knew I had to pray to understand what the plan was. It was not until I stepped outside of His will for my life and thought out the plan that I had finally come to know and understand God. It was a journey that I had embarked upon, and now with a little more knowledge of who God is in my life and what God wants for my life, I can gladly say, "I Will Go, Lord."

This change was not an overnight process. God and I fought many nights, and we often stopped speaking. If I told you that I wasn't upset, I'd be lying. We are shown that it is wrong to get mad at God, which it is; however, it does happen. It happened to me. One minute I was mad and then the next I said, "Your will be done in my life." I was mad at God because I felt like He had abandoned me. He let this man rape me, and He let this man get away with everything. I never took into account that this pit I was in, God was in it with me. His Word says, "I will not leave you nor forsake you." Deuteronomy 31:6. It took the knowledge of really studying to understand this journey. It took lots and lots, and probably more tears to accept this journey. I never wanted to write this book. It hurt too much to put just about all these words to paper. Despite my disobedience, God kept showing me the need for me to write it. He would not let me have a moment's rest. Each day that I woke, God would help me align the chapters so that they would be in order. He would also show me the pain of other people and help me to understand why this journey was what it was, and why there was a need for this process.

The process was never something that I would have acknowledged. I could have hidden my actions after the fact in my heart forever, but God would never allow it. I am forever strengthened by this process that He has taken me through. Had I not gone through this, I would have never known how strong I really am. I would not have known how strong I can be. Upon the final actions of this rape, I saw my life come to an end. Remember, I had thought something like this would kill me. I thought that if this ever happened to me, my life would be over. God knew how I felt, and He might have allowed this to happen to me, as well as Job and his unfortunate events, all for our revelation. It wasn't I who created the heavens or the earth. It is not I who created each human being and their unique fingerprint. Was it I who fills my own lungs with air, or is it I who causes my own heart to beat and pump blood throughout my body? Who wakes me each day? Maybe it was the alarm clock that I can take credit for setting because I was awakened to a morning of new mercies. No, each detail down to each second was and has always been orchestrated by our Almighty Father.

During my Job moment, I wish I could say that I had acted so good. I trusted God to redeem me and take care of me as I wanted Him to, but that is not what happened. The tears that I cried could probably fill up an Olympic-size swimming pool, and the hurt that I experienced caused so much anger that I had no idea how to shake it from me, not to mention the loss of my faith. I lost three years of my life because I was not prepared. I had been warned in the Bible to study to show thyself approved, and had not heeded its warnings. It was not until I found myself in the middle of these storms that I came to myself and realized that it was too late. I was not ready.

These events I questioned over and over for what seemed like three years kept me talking and waiting on God. I waited on His answers. It was easy to see the good in my life when everything was going right, but now the earth opened up, and it felt like all hell had broken loose. Now the birds never sang, and the sun never reached the top of the sky. I had been living in a constant state of darkness, and my mind was so focused on it. Time had begun to stand still for me. I had been stuck in a state of confusion, replaying the events for far too long. I had come to a point where there were no more tears left to cry, and it was time to take some form of action.

The darkness of my pain caused me to stay stuck watching the bad memories, replaying them over and over so I would sink further in despair. I didn't want to be in pain, nor did I want to replay the memories, but it was all I knew how to do. Caught up and living in my feelings was all that I knew at the moment. It was all about how I felt. It was all about the thoughts that had taken up residence in my reality, transferring me to the amazing state of limbo where I did nothing but think on them. The best way to describe it is, "It was a war raging inside myself that never went away."

Finally, I began to do the only thing I knew how to do. I started with the basics, what they teach in Bible school as a little child. I began to pray. Each time a bad thought crept in my mind, I started to pray. It was the action that I so hopelessly needed. You see the devil and his minions have only one purpose, and that is to ruin our relationship with God, or to keep us from a relationship with God. He tries his best to keep us focused on the bad, the wronged, and the confusion. In doing so, we are held from the truth. We are so focused on what was and what happened, instead of what is. Then we assume that we are so good and that we must be relieved from the hurt because of who we are and not what we are meant to do. Our enemies will take advantage of any opportunity to turn us away from God and make us question His love for us. I sat for years questioning, "Why me?" Over and over I questioned God. I allowed the enemy into my thoughts and world, and not only did he make me question God, but he also made me question myself. He has the ability to bring you to the ledge and then ask you, "So what are you going to do? Go ahead and jump!" By ledge, I am not only talking about suicide. It can figuratively mean anything—cheating, lying which in turn causes the loss of a job, murder—anything. And after he takes you to the ledge and proposes the question to you, you feel trapped. You're trapped not only because of your initial reaction, but also because the walk back from the ledge can be just as bad. I had compromised my workplace not only because I chose to love up on Sinister, but I already knew what they meant when they say, "You don't play where you work." It can mess up the way you earn money and make a living for your family. I had to go to work each day and see their faces knowing what they had done. The place I took refuge in initially, my job, had now mirrored my home. Now society and Sinister's friends look at him like he's the man and I'm some poor unfortunate soul. In some more text, his friends called me a fair-weathered friend. There was no longer any justification in what I had done, nor what he had done. I had to go to God and repent, ask for forgiveness of my sins that had been hidden or revealed. I had to go back to God.

Lord...I'm Truly Blessed

Finally brothers and sisters, whatever is true, whatever is noble, whatever is right, whatever is pure, whatever is lovely, whatever is admirable: If anything is praiseworthy: think about such things. Philippians 4:8

It could have been me...the one who God had not woken up this morning. Like some, we would like to give credit to the alarm clock, but there were some yet who still set their clocks and did not wake up. God could have easily said, "It is finished, the work I have for you; it is time to come on home." After Craig was done, God could have called my name. I could not look at what He did or had done for me because I was distracted. I couldn't count my blessings. The shock of what happened to my son, and the pain of what happened to me, held my focus solely on everything that had gone wrong. It was time to take account of my blessings. I had to look at the road ahead of me and stop looking in the rearview mirror.

God kept us safe. He did this for me and my family.

He could have let Craig put a hole in my son's head, and Gabriel could have died, but he didn't. Amid the chaos and confusion of that day, He commanded His angels concerning Gabriel to guard him carefully. Luke 4:10.

God could have let me stop breathing while Craig's hands were around my neck, but He didn't.

God could have let me run over my child that day when I barely knew Him, but He didn't.

God could have let me not have any clothes to wear, or shoes on my feet, but His blessings keep coming my way.

I could have no food on my table, in my refrigerator, or money to buy at the grocery store, but He has blessed me still.

I could be living in the streets at this very moment, or living in my car, but I have a home, a bed, covers to sleep under, and a place to wash my face.

I could still be in my storm suffering, tormented by the enemy every day, hurting, but I am blessed to have walked out.

I could still be in some dead-end relationship not knowing real love, not aware of the actions of others and their true nature and intentions for me, but I have the God-given discernment that I prayed for.

I could be dead in my sin, not knowing the true love of God.

I have been blessed, and my blessings outweigh my bad. I know it's easy to look at the wrongs that happen, because I had done it for so long. I was focused, my eyes fixated on the trouble that was circling me like vultures, but I had to intentionally see the good that was going for me. It had been a long road of hurt and frustration, but there were no more tears to cry. I had to take account of what was, not what I had lost. God will never use what you lost to bless you. If you take an account, the bad will never outweigh the good.

Soon, I had gone around my house putting up Post-it notes to encourage myself. I placed scriptures on my bathroom mirror, in the kitchen, and also on my bedroom walls. I chose anything that would lift me up. I stopped talking to Sinister, Ivy, and Craig. Anything that stopped my joy, I stopped doing. There was no time for fake anything. I coveted the relationships that brought me joy and the people that I knew were meant to be in my life. I prayed, prayed, and did more praying, and when I didn't understand, I prayed to understand. I also asked for prayers as well, but only from the people who I knew would pray for me.

Sometimes, you ask for prayer, and people say okay, but they never pray for you. I had to be intentional with my love. 1 Corinthians 13 is my favorite chapter in the Bible. It is ok to be patient, kind, and not envy others. I had to choose to love others intently, even those who hurt me. I realized one of the best things to do for each one of them was to let them all go, completely. For the sake of my sanity I had to love myself as well. It was time to heal. I had to keep telling myself again and again, "The bad does not outweigh the good!" I had to choose to love myself and get better anyway that I could. I had to change my heart and my mind, not only for myself, but also for my children whom God had placed in my care.

Lord...I'm Focused

I had always known the voice of God. The first time I had heard it was when I almost ran over my child. For almost three years He woke me up and said, "Good Morning."

My reply, "Leave me alone. I'm not talking to you."

"Write the book," He'd say next.

As mad as I was, I couldn't help but marvel in the voice of God. The wonder that He has purposed me for. Could this be what He spoke of when He said, "Before I formed you in the womb I knew you; before you were born I sanctified you; I ordained you a prophet to the nations."? Jeremiah 1:5. The easiest thing to do would be to walk away from God and what He had purposed me to do. To keep putting Him off and act like the Bible never existed, and to chase the words away that were locked in my heart.

Now, I can understand how people commit suicide. I can understand why people turn away from God. I can understand why the world thinks that God doesn't exist. I can understand why people choose in a split second to pull the trigger and take someone's life. I can understand how someone can stay lost in sin and how they hurt. I can understand why people judge others. I can understand the anxiety, the trauma of losing a loved one and then blaming it on God. I can understand how marriages stay stagnant for so long with no relief. I can understand why people cheat, and why they keep cheating. I can finally understand. Without limiting God, I can understand why. I can appreciate the hand of God and how it relates to my life. I can understand my enemy and his plan for my life. I can understand how my life has meaning and how my children's lives have meaning. I can understand the depth of God's love for me and my family. I can understand that I will not know or understand everything and that is perfectly fine with me. Ultimately, I know that I will never be able to completely understand God and His ways. There is a Creator, even if we decide to think otherwise. Our decision to believe in Him or not to believe in Him does not negate His existence. It is our finite thinking that causes us to lose out on the gifts that God has for us.

I could have stayed angry at God as if it would have changed a single piece of my past to help my future. As if the pot has a right to argue with his Creator. Isaiah 45:9. Who am I to tell God the direction that I should go, or the type of life that I should live? How can I presume to be so wise that I could tell God the directions that I will and won't take? "Girl, bye," could have been His reply, BUT God! "The Lord is merciful and gracious, slow to anger and abounding in mercy." Psalm 103:8. God my Creator, the one who has woven every intricate detail, from the birds in the sky to the depths of the sea and left no detail undone has left no stone unturned, and has left a manual as a guide of which we should choose to adhere to.

Yes, I had amazed myself to think I was as wise as I thought I was, and all on account of my pain. Could I go before God on the day of judgment and say, "I chose a new direction because He let me suffer."? Could I go before God and say, "God, it was all your fault because you didn't save me"? Certainly not. The steps of a good man are ordered. Psalm 37:23. Every move we make is ordered by God. Whether I was right or wrong in your eyes, only God can judge. Whether you are right or wrong, only God can judge you, and thank God because we are all flawed in our judgment.

It was a long journey to this point with God. I spent a significant amount of my time stewing with the enemy because my life was not where I wanted it to be. I wasted so much energy conversing with the devil as I presumed he and his minions laughed at my tears. I was so angry with God and the pain. It took time to recover, and soon I learned to quiet the enemy and listen to the voice of God. It was not until I began to listen to the voice of God that my life started anew. It was a little harder to hear, but I had already heard it. I just wasn't listening. Shamefully, I had decided what was best for me.

Clearly seeing the error of my ways, even if it was divinely ordained and interjected in my life, I can finally say Thank you Lord for not allowing me wallow in my self-pity and to sin any longer. Thank you Lord, for not allowing me stay in a place that could have eventually caused me, as well as the others who see me, to believe as I had. The time I spent pushing God away because I really didn't understand His ways or honestly know Him was a road that I wish I can say was not necessary, but it was. I thought I knew God. I thought I knew His plans for my life, even though I did not ask. I thought my life was my own and I could do with it as I pleased. The time that I spent sitting in the thick of it, allowing the darkness to engulf me, I didn't know how to cry out to God. In my wilderness, I sat waiting, wavering in faith and questioning every inch of God's love for me. I had even wondered if this had been my punishment for cheating. Among the many, many questions, I was always told that you don't question God. Even so, that morbid question still lingered—"why me?" And a fear of the earth opening up to taste my flesh was not enough to make me fear not asking God. It was not my intention to anger God. I just wanted to understand. My wilderness experience could have been 40 years like the children of Israel, and somehow it was cut short by 37 years. I could still be in my pain, crying every single day, but I'm not. I know there are some of you who have been dealing with issues for such a long time, but don't give up, and definitely don't give up on God. Ask Him to show you your enemies and show you His plan for your life. However, let me warn you - if you don't mean it, don't ask it.

Time to Renew My Mind

For every problem in our lives there is a purpose that we don't see, and a solution that is divinely at work. If I had seen any of this coming my way, and if I had known, I would have probably run and asked God to get someone else.

After realizing the issues that I had decided to take action against, and with the Bible as my guide, I began to think of the things that were going right as much as I possibly could. Being raped, going to the hospital, talking with the policeman, seeking help, and being laughed at by my so-called friends, have and will stay forever in my mind. I had wished I could rip those memories from my hippocampus, but they are necessary. I I recall the earlier events when I thought my mind was broken, and the cycle of hurt would not stop playing over and over and I wanted to give up, but God would not allow me stay where I was. Each thought brought me closer to Him because each time I thought on the bad, I prayed, and each time the enemy caused me stress, I sang. I listened to gospel, I read books, I prayed some more, and I chose a new life. I did my absolute best to keep God in the forefront of my mind so the enemy would no longer have a foothold. I refused to give him any more room to run around causing trouble with my thoughts. Removing the stress that other people caused me changed my life and helped me concentrate on the good things that were happening. Instead of looking at the bad in every situation, I did my best to see the good in it, and it helped me get to where I am today. The battle back to God was an uphill one, but I did it!

During the second visit with the psychologist, I asked her to help me shut the bad memories out of my mind. I told her that I wanted to forget all of them. She smiled at me and said, "You will never be able to forget what has happened to you. We can try to change our association of the bad thoughts, as well as working on the triggers, and in time you will be able to cope a little bit better. However, I want you to look at it this way; your mind is very powerful - it can take you back to certain places and times with the mere whiff of a flower, or by hearing a song from your past. It is the same for bad memories. They will never go away; but in time the events can fade." Sitting and listening to her made me sick and angry all at the same time, but I was determined to get the help that would fix me. I was determined to make changes in my life that would allow me to live a better and more productive life. I had gotten to the point where I was sick and tired of crying. Honestly, there were no more tears left. I was "All Cried Out" as Lisa Lisa sang in her song.

Educating Myself

I had to renew my mind. I had to change the way I thought, and the only way to begin was to educate myself on my issues. The psychologist said I had PTSD. Post-Traumatic Stress Disorder was just the beginning. It was time to understand what this disorder was about. I already knew why I had it, and now I had to educate myself so that I could get better. Post-Traumatic Stress Disorder is a mental health condition triggered by a terrifying event, per the definition given by Mayoclinic.org. Some symptoms include severe anxiety, nightmares, and flashbacks, as well as uncontrolled thoughts about an event.

PTSD symptoms are also grouped into four different types:

Intrusive memories, avoidance, negative changes in thinking and mood, and changes in physical and emotional reactions. The symptoms are not set in stone to any particular person, nor will they come at any specific time. These symptoms can even start years after the initial event, and as I began to educate myself to try and get better, I was relieved to know that I wasn't going crazy. I just had to come up with a plan to help myself get better one day at a time, one second at a time even. I had spent the previous three years learning a new behavior, and now it was time to change my thought process once more. I was looking over my shoulder, expecting more harm to come my way. Locked up in a state of depression because things were not where or how I wanted them to be. It had to stop if I wanted to get better. My next step was to read. Read as much as I possibly could. I started with the Bible because I was once told that everything we have gone through or could go through is in the Bible. Solutions to life's problems are found chapter by chapter, and all I had to do was open it and read it for myself.

Educating myself on what was going on in my life ignited a change in me that helped me see things from a new perspective. Had I not wanted, or tried to educate myself, I could still be stuck in the same depressed state that I originally started, and although it took me three years to lift a finger, I'm glad I started from somewhere. Les Brown said in a seminar, "You don't have to be great to get started, but you have to start if you want to be great." So with one foot in front of the other, I began.

Have a Battle Buddy

After renewing my mind, educating myself on what was happening to me, and choosing to get better, I needed someone who I could count on to help me get to my new destiny. Someone I could hold accountable to help me, and it just so happened to be my husband, Chris. He was the one who kept me from the ledge most days. When I first opened up to him about what happened, he told me that no matter the time of day, I could call him, and we could talk. His exact words were, "I'll never get tired of listening to you. I'll never get tired of talking about this with you. Any time, day or night you call me, because I'm here for you." He would sit and listen to me kick, cry and scream, and no matter what time, we would talk. He never got tired of listening to me, he never got tired of the tears, and he never told me to just hurry up and get over it. Chris took the time to pray for me, and with me. I cried so many nights, and he let me get it all out; he was the one who kept me going and I didn't even know it. He was my battle buddy. I knew I could count on him to be there for me and with me. As the friends who were supposed to be there were rerouted, I had a select few that I knew were going to be in the trenches with me. Besides my husband

Chris, it was only going to be two other people: Michelle my sister, and Michelle my sister in Christ. They were the ones who I was blessed to have in my life. If it had not been for God placing these three people in my life, I don't know how things would have turned out. We all need someone to talk to, and they helped me get through most of my troubled nights. I am, and will always be, forever grateful to God that He placed them in my life just in the nick of time.

No one should ever go it alone. Ecclesiastes 4:9-12; and after I prayed for better friends, God blessed me with three great ones. My sister Michelle would call me just when my brain would go into overdrive and I was stressed beyond measure. Michelle, my sister in Christ, would pray for me and with me, all while Chris kept me talking. These people never made me feel less than, they never made me question their love for me, and I knew that if there was anything I needed, I could count on them. They encouraged me, prayed for me, listened to me cry many nights, and never once said, "Oh just get over it."

In the course of this world, changing who I associate myself with helped me get better. Had I stayed attached to some of my other friends, I would still be depressed. These were the people that I was getting advice from. The other people didn't care to see what was going on in my life, and I don't blame them. I can forgive each one of them because it is this offense that has shown me who is reliable and who is not, who was supposed to be in my life and who wasn't. There is no reason to get mad at any one of them. I can easily accept and know that I am not supposed to be friends with everyone. I made a joke on Facebook once that my circle is so small now that I can't even see it. I have just learned to make better choices when it comes to the people who I choose to spend the rest of my days with. Forty years have gone by so quickly for me, and I no longer have time to keep making the same mistakes with the same people.

Pray

Lastly, I prayed! I prayed and talked to God and let Him know exactly how I felt. When I had my closet moment, alone on the floor, God and I had some words. I didn't go to God and say, "God, here I am as humbly as I know how." I didn't pray like some of the proper people in the church with the hither, thither, and thous. My simplest prayer was, "God I need your help!" I talked to God like He was my long lost friend who I hadn't seen in a long time. I just began to talk with Him daily. Mostly because He was talking to me, but also because I needed His help. He was the only one that would be able to help me get through the hurt that I carried with me for so long.

Praying begins to open up communication with God, and what better way to get help for the troubles we are facing than to ask the Creator to help us? Psalm 107:28-30. I spent so many nights not seeking God's help because I was mad, and it caused me to stay stationed in my storm. I didn't care one way or the other about talking to God because of my anger. I had not realized that for the enemy to attack my mind and thoughts, I had to allow him access to me, and I allowed him access through my anger. I let him change my views of God, and what I knew was immediately replaced, infected by a new perspective. I saw God as some mean God that just wanted to punish me, and not Craig. I saw God as unfair, and not just as it says in the Bible. It took more nights and more days to walk with Him, lots of reading to get to know Him and the Love that He does have for us all. In the beginning, I was set to stay fastened to a belief that God was not Almighty or all-powerful simply because He refused to help me out of my situation.

In my mind, I was comfortable to allow the enemy change each and every thought, all on account of my hurt, shame, misconception, and fear.

Praying opened up the doors of communication between God and I once more. It opened up my heart and mind once more to who God really is. In a book written by Stormie Omartian, *Prayer Warrior*, she goes in-depth on the power of praying and becoming a prayer warrior. Somewhere I had lost all this information and decided it best to concentrate on what was in front of me instead of what I knew. My focus was on my trouble, not on the God who could help me through my trouble. It was a cycle that I had repeated to no end for three years, and a hunger to get better so large that no one could feed — no one but God. I pushed God away for so long, and yet He was the one who I needed.

At the beginning of my relationship with Craig, I remember being so happy with him. Things were going so well. We were on the road to the white picket fence, two kids and a dog, or more like five kids and a dog. We had dreams of a blessed life, and it all came crashing down when he did the unthinkable to me. I have forgiven him for it, and I can even assume my child has also forgiven him, but it had caused a seismic shockwave in our lives and plotted a course that we were both not sure how to navigate. I had always said I could never be with someone who was beating on me, and that included my children. The fear of this continuing was worth me disconnecting and removing myself from the situation to keep my children safe from future events.

Sinister, Ivy and I were friends. They made it easy to come to work after everything that was going on at home. I can remember the good times we shared and the good people they are. Instead of staying stuck in my hurt and complaining why they hadn't been there for me, it had come to my understanding that they were only supposed to be in my life for a short time. I was only supposed to be in their lives for a short time. There were many things we taught each other and many things I can take with me that will help me in my future when it comes to friendships, and it was best learned now instead of later. It would hurt me more if I stayed in my feelings than if I had forgiven them and let them go. You see, I was supposed to feel every inch of this pain; the heat from these relationships was supposed to be turned up to scorching level because the door was closing so I would never go back. The intense pain I felt was supposed to remove me from these relationships and keep me from returning.

Staying angry with God could have been a tragic beginning to an end. My life would definitely have been over if I kept this type of mindset. I had searched the Bible for so long as to who God is; I searched the Internet, and I even asked some people who God was to them. In the end, it is who God is to me that matters. My hurt locked me up in a cage, and as I focused on it, I kept the pain alive. I kept the hurt pumping through my veins and the tears flowing. It was not God's fault that I had traveled down this road. It was not God's fault that life was the way it was.

My life was supposed to be this way. Everything happens for a reason, we hear. Life happens the way it's supposed to happen. God orchestrates the days and night, the ins and outs and the routes we should take. The *why* of it is always revealed, as long as we stay the course. I have finally stayed the course. I finally have the faith to push forward, to believe and trust that God wants me in this exact spot for a specific purpose. I have finally accepted that what has happened was supposed to happen, and even though it hurt like hell, God has kept me. He kept me safe during the whole process. I could have died, and my child could have died. My life could be so much worse, but I'm here.

After the hurt, and the shame of what had happened, I sat to meditate on my events. I am so much stronger for it happening, as much as I don't want to admit it. I am so much stronger for this man coming into my life and doing what he thought would hurt me. It was the only thing I was afraid of. It was the only thing that held me back from my purpose. I am not afraid anymore. I am not ashamed of this anymore, and there is only One to be grateful for and to. To God be the glory for showing me my weakness, allowing me to go through the anger and the pain, and helping me come through it all. Now I see the God who I serve.

There may be something that you are fighting with. There may be some scares that hold you back from your purpose; whatever it may be - and I know it is hard to - let go. The hurt and the pain may be hard to let go of, but you must try to move forward from the pain. Don't let the enemy plot a course for you as he did me for so long. Don't let the hurt keep you stuck as it did me. It took me way more time than I ever want anyone to know, all on account of my anger. It is time to welcome God back into your life and find out why your life is the way it is, and how it can be better. You simply have to ask and wait for the reply. We must learn to be patient with God. He has waited for us for so long, and we must be as equally patient with Him. Your best life is ahead of you. Cry your tears, take your good days with your bad days, but never stop moving forward. The good will outweigh the bad; it always does.

I can identify with the fact that so many of us live with some level of doubt, fear, depression, and anxiety; however, the God I had come to understand and finally know for myself can and will deliver us from it all. We must keep in mind that the devil is not out to destroy your past. He is not looking to destroy your present. His job is to destroy your future, and the future of those who you can touch. The people you have the ability to make smile and the people you can help God save.

Now I say proudly, "It is good for me that I have been afflicted, that I may learn your statutes. Psalm 119:71. I have learned to trust in the Lord with all my heart, and not lean on my own understanding. In all my ways I acknowledge Him as He makes straight my path. Proverbs 3:5-6. I have learned to Rejoice in hope, be patient in tribulation, and be constant in prayer. Romans 12:12.

"The greater your knowledge of the goodness and Grace of God on your life, the more likely you are to praise Him in the storm" -Matt Chandler

The Lord says, "Now, therefore, listen to me, my children, for blessed are those who keep my ways. Hear instructions and be wise, and do not disdain it. Blessed is the man who listens to me, watching daily at my gates, watching the posts of my doors. For whoever finds me finds life, and obtains favor from the Lord, but he who sins against me wrongs his own soul; all those who hate me love death."

Proverbs 8:32-36

THE

END

CPSIA information can be obtained
at www.ICGtesting.com
Printed in the USA
LVHW090211261121
704503LV00008B/45